In MotherWords

Unconventional Wisdom For Moms Raising Daughters

Marty Burns Wolfe   Foyne Mahaffey   Laura Manthey

IN MOTHERWORDS

Unconventional Wisdom For Moms Raising Daughters

Carroll & Graf Publishers, Inc.
New York

First edition 1996.

Carroll & Graf Publishers, Inc.
260 Fifth Avenue
New York, NY 10001

ISBN 0-7867-0328-8

Library of Congress Cataloging-in-Publication data is available.

Manufactured in the United States of America.

Thanks to Cait who after eleven measly years has figured out what it took me four long decades to fully understand

Don't give up
Don't be a quitter
And while you're at it
Don't be bitter.

– *Foyne*

Thanks to
Katherine R. Weishaar
who imparted her wisdom
and encouragement
to me in eighth grade,
knowing that serving
detentions for
constructively belligerent
illustration would
eventually lead to
profitability.

– *Laura*

Thanks to those who ignored, aggravated and encouraged us. To those who asked for a free copy, the answer is still no. Love and luck to Danielle, Brittany, Lauren, Jamie and Schu.

– *Marty*

TABLE OF CONSCIENCE

"Let your conscience be your guide." said Jimminy Cricket.

It always sounds profound and easy, until you really think about it. Where does a good conscience come from? Individually, one could guess, we get it from our parents who got it from their parents and their parents and their parents who got it from, ultimately, the first person to not eat her vegetables in front of a mother who knew a little geography.

You start out eating the peas because you are told to and then as time goes on you eat them because starving children don't have them, because they have protein, so they don't go to waste or to prevent hurting the cook's feelings. That's a sophisticated jump. We learn with good parenting that more important than our own preferences are issues of responsibility, well-being and human kindness. Good parenting ought to result in children who not only eat their vegetables, but request and share them with others.

As adults, we ought to make decisions based on what is good for us and good for others. In the tough times, when what is good for us is hurtful to others, we have only enforceable law and our consciences to guide. Without a foundation set with a mixture of respect, loyalty, honesty, and fairness, one has only enforceable law to steer him down the straight and narrow. And imposed conscience is an oxymoron.

Children who have a conscience are the ones with the report cards reading, "Plays well with others. Shares. Shows good cooperation and leadership skills." They become the teens who admit to love and are protective of their families, are involved in community service and show signs of compassion. They become "outwardly mobile" in their efforts to follow the voices inside them. They have a clear sense of right and wrong. They become the adults we respect and rally around, then turn to for counsel and advice. They become the bosses who care deeply for their employees and show it. They are the speakers who are careful with their words, the spouses who bring out the best in one another and the parents honored. The circle is complete, the world one link stronger.

If we consciously raise our children, teach them to listen to their own, and show by example how a good conscience followed is a powerful force, they will come upon a positive and profitable future, not by luck. We're starting with girls.

Hey, it's hard to know where to begin when you're out to change the world. So we decided to let our consciences be our guides.

CONTENTS

INTRODUCTION

When was the last time you thought, "I sound just like my mother!" Check your watch.

It may be thoughtful confession after admonishing your own daughter, strong and able, for putting her elbows on the table.

It's a retort of last resort when "because I said so" doesn't work. It's the white flag ending of the fashion standoff when "Are you going out like that?" is the best you can come up with. You have surrendered, moaning and shaking, heads in hands. But take heart.

Mothers do speak a language remembered. We hold those voices in our heads as we perform brilliantly and badly throughout our lives. We hear those words when we consider giving up and don't. We hear them when we almost put an eye out or smack our gum. We hear them as we tell white lies, when we get blue ribbons, too big for our britches, or stood up. We hear it when we French kiss and although not always moved to stop, we at least think about it.

In other words, MotherWords are powerful. They are the pats on the back and the raps on the knuckles. They keep us in tow. They keep us going. But the new millennium calls for new techniques combined with traditional wisdom. As daughters we have tasted adventure, smelled success and are feeling demands Grandma never imagined. It's time to memo, fax and e-mail our very best, prying hinges off doors so our daughters have easier access.

For those of us who occasionally sound just like our mothers, but generally aren't thinking like them, it's time to hold hands, take their reins, grab the torches and pass along the future's best MotherWords.

The WONDERBRA

I work in a television newsroom as a newscaster. One night the producer, a bright young woman, asked me to look at some videotape that had come down on the satellite feed from the network. She wanted to rework a story on the "WonderBra" and put it into the 10 o'clock newscast.

I thought she was kidding. I searched her expression for a hint of humor–a twinkle, a grin, a wink, a wrinkle. Enough time elapsed to punctuate the point that this was not going to turn into a moment of female bonding. She was dead serious. I met her reach and accepted the videotape (the way a child takes a forkful of spinach) and headed for the tape machine. A minute-twenty later I knew we were in trouble. Here was a story with a lot of close-up shots of lacy bras on beautiful young women brandishing brand-new cleavage. It was a revolutionary design – complex construction and fifty-two separate pieces of fabric and elastic. Those few facts were all the reporter had managed to get into the story and these in no way obscured the true mission of the multimedia blitz: show half-naked women in sexy lingerie while surreptitiously advertising the product, boosting sales and manipulating a visual medium hungry for provocative stories that evoke response.

Now having been in the broadcast business for years I can recognize a good story when it strolls by, but this one had trouble written all over it. Trouble with a capital "T" and that stands for titillation. This was the kind of videotape that incites the normally nice people who call our switchboard to complain they're just fed up with the trash on TV. They are often the same folks who call when a Presidential news conference interrupts their soapy sex-opera.

This simple little story was going to polarize an audience already looking for any video on which to hang an argument. It just wasn't worth it. It was a story custom fit for a tabloid show but not in the league with the Middle East Peace Accord, a good five-alarm fire, or even the closing average of the Dow Jones. This story clearly was not worth a minute-twenty of the pitiful twelve minutes devoted to the events that shook our little planet that day. Then I did something no good journalist should ever let happen or at least admit. I objected on personal grounds. I didn't want to run the story because I thought it inappropriate, sexist and stupid. I was offended but it was clear I stood alone in this feminist forest looking around for someone to support me. I knew the "F" word was going to creep into the discussion and escalate a little philosophical skirmish into a battle

and sexuality. Yeah, yeah, yeah. For me this story did not justify putting tits on TV.

Being a dutiful employee and ever mindful of the anchor/producer relationship, I tried to find an uninflammatory way of voicing my opinions without compromising my position. What came out was, "Why on earth, except for titillation, would you run this?" She smirked. "It's big news." At that point I could see it was a larger problem than the double-breasted videotape dilemma. Here before me stood a self-reliant and self-assured woman who saw no reason not to run the story.

between anchor and producer. I accepted the fact that I was going to have to be a conscientious objector.

Had the story been about a revolutionary design for a "Wonder Jock" it might have made the wire services but you can bet your double "D" it wouldn't have been videotaped with close-up shots of before and after. Our producer was proposing to put on TV the *Cosmo* cover image of breast perfection and that flew in the face of my convictions. Women are more than the sum of their body parts and must be valued and respected for things other than appearance

In that flash of a moment I saw the vast gap between generations staring me in the face. There was no way I could expect her to understand that I was part of a movement that had burned perfectly good bras on the fires of higher reason. A generation that had marched on capitols and carried placards. A generation that still believed feminist was a label worth sticking to. The two decades between us wasn't the problem. It was our experiences that created the chasm, and at that moment the great divide was on videotape.

I heard the loading of guns. She said to me, "I want to run the story, and I want you to be the one to write and read it. To have Jerry do it might appear sexist." The battle's first bomb dropped.

Jerry, my co-anchor, enjoyed this little diatribe. He has never been one to shy away from a good argument, especially one between two women. Only half-jokingly he has used the term "femi-nazi" and always with the intent of sparking a reaction. He offered up the observation that if we were going to run the WonderBra story then writing and reading it should be my job. He said that the audience would accept it better coming from me, a woman and all, but he left out the fact that by my doing so, he would be off the hook.

I realized he clearly understood why this was troublesome for me and he had every intention of sitting back and watching the implosion.

I wrote the story, beginning with a ten-second on-camera shot of both of us, with me recounting the "discussion" over running it, followed by something of a personal disclaimer of responsibility. From there we ran the videotape, showing the least revealing medium distance shots of the "body wear" revolution in the making. The "story" lasted about thirty seconds and was delivered with dispassionate disinterest. I was piqued with a purpose but had fought the good fight and lost.

The second bomb dropped when Jerry, silent throughout the story looked straight into the camera and chimed, "I didn't care whether we ran the story as long as we ran the pictures." A grin. He had upped the ante and he knew it. My mouth smiled and I read the tease to the commercial break that the newsroom phones would be ringing. I was wrong.

When the show was over, the producer punched the button on the control room console and sang through my earpiece that not one person had called the newsroom to complain. She was flaunting her vindication. It was clear I had been oversensitive to

a non-issue and, because no one called, she was off the hook.

I had carried the banner right over the border into "femi-nazi" land" and found myself without an army.

For the next few days, I spent most of my non-airtime answering letters. Most were thoughtful, articulate and emotional and came from both men and women. Some writers were totally outraged, some disappointed, others shocked at "that bra story" in the newscast. The disgruntled penned, "I will never watch your news again." Those I surmised were the sex-opera viewers. A couple of chastising letters were from women who assumed it was my choice to include the story. They had clearly missed the sarcasm in my delivery. They didn't see the tongue stuck in my cheek. However, most were sympathetic and agreed that the story was an affront to our gender; sexist, demeaning and inappropriate.

I answered every viewer, taking great solace in the words of the insightful woman who wrote "How dare you make that nice girl read that horrible tripe?" With the exception of the world "girl" I concurred. I kept the gloating to myself but gave the producer some letters to answer. By the next week the newsroom focus had shifted from brassieres to balanced budgets. Life moved on.

But the media manipulation worked. WonderBras popped up everywhere. And true to capitalist form, there are knockoffs everywhere. Retailers couldn't keep them in stock. They sold like hot...pants. Now they're "on sale" everywhere.

The point here is not brassieres or marketing or media. It is enlightenment. That young female producer is bright, capable, hardworking and earnest, but in some very important ways I believe she isn't enlightened. She wasn't around for the struggles of the "campaign."

I hope she will re-examine some of the not-so-simple things that deserve questioning. We need sure and steady beats, coming from many directions. For without the banging of the drum every now and then I worry that the sounds we need to hear will not be made.

A drum roll, please...

THE FIRST TEN YEARS
ARE THE HARDEST

Reflections on your daughter's early years

The time to think about all of this is before the first ultrasound. Before the first thoughtful friend brings you a Baby's Name book, before the doctor says "It's a girl!" Throw down the pacifier and accept this challenge: Try picking out a name that doesn't scream boy or girl. Try:

Francis or **Frances?**

Pretty androgynous. Could be a boy. Could be a girl. You have to admit it's a weird name for a baby but what's weirder is that it is hard to find names that won't gender-type, a name that doesn't tell someone whether to give you a pink blanket or a blue one.

I wonder what would happen if children were given names that were non-gender specific. Would Ralph grow up differently from Rosemary if both names were given to boys and girls? Maybe not, but there is no denying we treat children differently based on their gender.

Back in the '60s, despite the blue haze swirling around their heads, some hip parents caught on to that. They avoided the gender-typing and labeled their kids with names that will be forever linked to the Age of Aquarius. Excluding Moonglow and the like–names any child would gladly relinquish upon reaching the age of consent–there are a lot of kids out there named Taylor instead of Tyler or Mackensie instead of Michael. There are Seans and Shauns and Shawns. No clues.

As a Martha turned Marty, and a Foyne, there is a definitive difference in the kinds of mail addressed to us. We get a lot of stuff for Mr. Burns-Wolfe or Mr. Mahaffey. Maybe if Marty were Martina and Foyne were Foyni things would be different but "i's" and "y's" send signals, too. Sort of the letter versus chromosome difference. You can call a girl Billy, but unless your friends, family and neighbors know it's a girl, they'll assume it's a boy. You can call a boy Toni, but unless they know it's a boy, they'll assume it's a girl.

So be advised. If you call your daughter Bobbi, Randi, Ricki, Sandi, Terri, Jerri, Kerri, Micki, she's only one chromosome and one letter away from being a Bobby, Randy, Ricky, Sandy, Terry, Jerry, Kerry or Mickey, but she's still labeled.

If you think none of this matters and we don't label our children, don't judge their potential, don't categorize their behavior or raise them according to what's expected of their gender, then examine what pops into your mind when you read these names: Robin, Glenn, Chris, Jamie, Alex, and Blaire.

See, no clues.

Try naming your child before the ultrasound. It's a liberating idea.

Picking a name is just the start of a mother's maternal awakening. Consider these:

Thoughts on passages through the first decade.

✱ Resist identifying your baby by the color of her clothes. Give no visual clues. Societal clues keep shifting, anyway. Hey, before 1950 most baby boys were dressed in pink, girls in blue. Was there mass gender confusion before the color-coding shifted again? What power, color? It's almost 2000. How about paisley?

✱ When your newborn cries in the middle of the night wake your partner even and especially if you're nursing. Both of you should stay awake together, the same amount of time. Reject the tired argument that at least one parent ought to be rested. Pretend you are both lactating! This is the only way to prevent the possibility of later and certain resentment.

As she grows give her gifts like batteries, wire, bulbs, nails, boards, screws and screwdrivers and hammers. You may be the only one and she'll thank you when she's on her own trying to hang a picture in the dark.

✤ Recognize it's time to teach your daughter how to work the washer and dryer when she begins each morning complaining about not having anything clean to wear.

1.   2.   3.   4.   5.   6.   7.

✱ Start to give your daughter little choices early in life, a written menu for breakfast for example. Along with learning to read, she'll learn to make decisions and learn to take them seriously. Then teach her how to make the breakfast as well as a choice.

✱ Don't buy your daughter dolls unless they wet, cry or scream unpredictably and uncontrollably. Children aren't quiet. Dolls shouldn't be either. It's unrealistic.

✱ When your daughter is angry with you and yells "I hate you" just look at her and say sweetly, "Well, I love you." It works.

✗ Avoid criticisms of things your daughter can't change. For example, "Why do you part your hair down the middle when you have a nose like that?"

In your darkest hours, when your child has just come home with purple hair and a nose ring, picture both of you thirty years from now and know that this too shall pass.

Prepare yourself for the onslaught of folks who believe that as a new mom you know nothing and need all the help you can get. There will be helpful advice, well-meaning but unsolicited, and some of it will deserve:

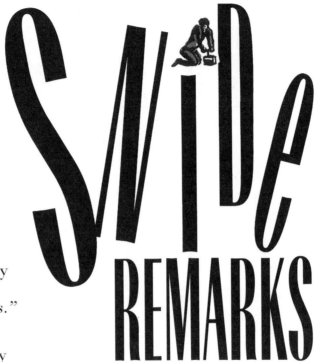

SNIDE REMARKS

When your friends ask if Alex is potty trained yet, smile and say: *"If Alex is still in diapers on prom night, then I'll worry."*

When your toddler is throwing a loud, rolling-around, screaming, stomping, nasty tantrum, simply inform observers: *"It must be the steroids."*

When grandparents ask why Pat isn't using a spoon yet, you might respond: *"Actually, I'm surprised Pat is even using her fingers to eat that. At home we eat with our feet."*

When your daughter shows no manners, look down your nose and state: *"I'm grooming her for aristocracy."*

When your children are fighting one another in a public place, state firmly: *"You just wait until I get you home to your mother!"*

When people say: "Oh, doesn't Terry speak yet?" look them straight in the eye and answer: *"We don't ever encourage Terry to speak. We hear that can really backfire on you."*

When they say, "Shy isn't she?" reply: *"No, just cerebral."*

When your child says, *"Do I have to?"* don't even answer.

You are going to run out of answers by the time your daughter reaches the age of two, better known as "The Inquisition." You will swear your little one is in training to be a reporter. "How" and "Why" become the building blocks of every conversation and your answers will begin to form a life-long perception. Overstating the case you say? Nope. There's a reason they call them:

The Terrible Twos

Experts in child development have spent years in research labs at universities all over the world watching our children. They enjoy it. They sometimes get published, even paid for their work. Here is some of what their research found:

Infants are born asexual, but by the age of two children have identified the sex roles of others. Boys recognize other boys, girls recognize other girls.

The majority of two-year-olds in a sex-role study gave pictures of sex-typed things such as irons, clothes dryers and purses to women in the study. Ties, carpenter's tools and lawn mowers went to the men. Sex role stereotyping starts early and we supply the tools.

POP!

What's terrible about the twos is that we're not giving little boys clothes dryers and irons and giving little girls carpenter's tools and lawn mowers.

From the outset of structured play and learning, little boys get more praise, more punishment, more attention from parents, teachers and everybody else. Girls learn to let boys get out front first.

We don't see it when girls are left hanging back, letting boys take the first steps. How can we wonder why little girls don't grow up believing they can be Presidents and Prime Ministers while boys consider it a birthright?

We wonder what Justice Ruth Bader-Ginsberg and Margaret Thatcher played with when they were kids.

21

So face it. Some things don't change because we don't change them. Think about it.
We all grow up mimicking what we know even when we despise it.

In Mother Words

You'll remember these things your mother said to you that you swore you'd never say if you ever had a daughter.
We've added the socially acceptable, politically correct versions translated into '90s speak and then
real-Mom translations of what they meant and mean still.

I don't care if Suzy's mother is letting her do it. I'm not Suzy's mother. If Suzy jumped off a bridge would you want to jump off a bridge, too?

Be an independent thinker. Weigh the pros and cons.

Suzy's mother is a wacko. I wish they'd move.

It didn't just get up and walk away!

You must take responsibility for your organizational problems.

You are such a slob.

Do you think money grows on trees?

We are having some cash flow problems at the moment.

You're old enough to be making your own spending money.

When you're paying the dental bills you can eat all the candy you want.

Until you're financially independent, consider your teeth rentals.

Stop eating so much junk!

Don't you use that tone of voice with me young lady...

Your passion is appreciated. Your sarcasm is not.

You're really close to being grounded.

If I've told you once I've told you a thousand times...

I'm looping.

I know you're ignoring me.

As long as you live under my roof you'll live by my rules.

Work with me on this...

You're too big to spank, but I can throw your independent butt out of this house.

Because I said so.

I'm not in the mood for arbitration.

I don't have to give you a reason, just do it.

I'm not asking you, I'm telling you!

Consider this a directive.

When I want your opinion, I'll give it to you.

Do you want me to pull this car over?

I'm growing weary of listening to your opinions.

I'm really losing it, but I can't reach you from the front seat.

If your head wasn't attached you would lose that, too.

You need a management system.

You're irresponsible. I'll be taking care of you forever.

When I was your age...

History has taught us...

If it was good enough for me, it's good enough for you.

You're acting just like your father.

Overcome your genetics.

I hate it when he does that, too.

I'll give you something to cry about!

This situation could escalate and I'm the one in control.

You think you've got it bad? I could have been a dancer.

Go ask your father. If he says it's OK, then it's OK with me.

Have you built a global consensus here?

I'm not going to be the one taking the blame when something goes wrong.

There's nothing funny about that.

Our senses of humor are divergent.

People are going to think we don't have any class!

It's only funny until someone loses an eye.

That's really rather humorous but if the consequences require medical attention, you're in big trouble.

Cut it out, now!

Is that what you're wearing?

Once again you've exercised your sartorial independence and creativity.

God, that's hideous.

You kids are eating me out of house and home!

Your healthy appetites are creating a financial burden on the family budget.

I was saving that for myself!

Listen here Lady Jane!

Let me enlighten you...

I'm so angry I can't even remember your first name!

I'm not saying this just to hear myself talk.

While I enjoy the sound of my own voice, my purpose here is twofold.

I sound like an idiot repeating this stuff over and over again.

Put on clean underwear. You never know when you'll end up in an accident.

Clean body wear makes you feel better about yourself.

People will think I don't do the laundry.

You'll understand this when you get older.

This concept may be too sophisticated at this time.

I haven't the slightest idea either.

Turn that down.

Please respect the space and personal needs of other family members.

I hate that crap. I wish I were alone.

I've given up everything for you kids.

Sacrifices for the sake of priorities are sacrifices well made.

I hate my first husband.

You're going to break your neck if you keep that up.

Think about the safety and wellness rules we have discussed.

I'm going to break your neck if you keep that up.

When you pay for your own apartment, you can decorate the way you want.

We value artistic expression in this family, but please remember, we are sharing this living space.

This is my house and don't you forget it.

Act like a lady!

Use your best manners, be quiet and do what you're told.

I want other parents to wish they had kids like you.

You're eating like there's no tomorrow.

As a responsible parent, I can assure you you'll never go hungry.

Do you eat like this when you're at other people's houses?

I hope you've learned something from this.

With experience comes wisdom.

Is this what it takes to get it through your thick skull?

You're the reason I have gray hair.

I'm very concerned about your well-being.

My looks are gone.

Don't make me tell you again.

At the risk of repeating myself, I'll just remind you of your obligations.

I know you heard me, now just do it.

Don't you get on your high horse with me, young lady!

Learning to elevate one's self is good, but respect for your elders is paramount.

What I say goes and don't you forget it.

I'll teach you a lesson you'll never forget.

This is something you need to understand from a parental perspective.

I'm not a violent person but I'm developing this twitch.

Do as I say, not as I do.

Let me verbalize your parameters.

Don't screw up your life like I screwed up mine.

I don't care if it's called a miniskirt. It's too short!

That is suggestive attire and totally inappropriate for someone your age.

You look like a tramp.

*Those mother words will be hard
to resist. So will Barbie, a mom's
first toy dilemma. You know you shouldn't but
your daughter pleads. Cajoles. Bribes. And you
can't blame her. She's "Bomb-Barbied" and
your resistance to the phenomenon will
evaporate as fast as the money in your wallet.
After all, she wants:*

The dream doll.

Barbie is a world-wide institution. The dream doll, designed by a woman but perfect for a man, is adored by millions of little girls who dress and undress her, by adults who collect them in their designer rags and by sociologists who wonder what Barbie-Mania is really all about.

That 11½ inch plastic paragon of beauty is now 35, has never married the only man she's ever dated, career hops, spends a fortune in hair coloring, never takes off her makeup and likes clothes with a lot of glitter on them. Think about it. She's a questionable role model at best.

But the more you tell your child (or yourself) that she shouldn't have a Barbie, or two or seven or sixteen, the more she'll want one and the more your relatives will see a need to provide her with one, or two, or seven or sixteen. So if she is like every other little girl and has to have her Barbies, then try slipping the following foreplay into her thoughts:

What does Ken do for a living? Who is this guy anyway? Does he have a job? Where did he get the money for the cool car? We suggest that unless he can answer the above questions, move on. He's probably the kind of guy your mother warned you about.

Consider the number of people you know who drive a pink car, live in a house with a pink roof and have a closet filled with clothes like Barbie's. Aside from the occasional Mary Kay rep, most women wouldn't consider the pink car, wouldn't buy a house with a pink roof and wouldn't want to dress that way. Dolly Parton is a possible exception, and she has other redeeming qualities.

Barbie is not every man's dream girl. Some men prefer brunettes. Look around whatever room you are in. How many bodies like Barbie's do you see? Keep in mind that if Barbie were a real woman, she wouldn't be able to menstruate because of her low body weight. Our guess is if you added her waist measurement to her hip measurement the total would still not equal her bust size!

Don't forget to add that Barbie is really a hardworking entrepreneur whose company is about to break into the Fortune 500, is close to her siblings, parents and friends, and keeps an inventory of her accessories on a database.

Insist her feet are pointed that way to symbolize forward motion and upward mobility.

There's always room for a little dream of your own.

Kids have dreams too, but we don't often listen to what they're trying to say. With a less than perfect command of the language they often speak volumes in simple, declarative sentences that fly right over our otherwise occupied minds. Sometimes it takes someone other than Mom to hear what's really being said. For one little girl it was telling her teacher:

"My goal is to build more."

Teaching first grade is a trip. Everything we as a society ever become is there. It's all there. The charity, the goodness, the enthusiasm, the innocence, the hierarchy, the territorialism...and the greed. It's natural at six to look out only for number one, but the chromosomes are all there and nothing brings out the worst in children, that primitive, raw, human greed, better than the division of goodies.

The goodies in my classroom were Legos. Parents, you know about Legos, those little plastic linking toys that hurt so much when you step on them barefooted at night?

I had a bunch of them available for my students to use at school. They were thrown together in a big box which I would lug out during choice time.

The requests came often and always from boys. I would check around the room as I carried the box slowly from the back of the room up to the carpet, providing ample opportunity for some girl to run up and ask if she could use them too. Didn't happen.

Report card time came around and I asked all the kids to think about a goal they wanted to reach in the next month or so. Spelling aside, these were well thought out serious goals.

I came upon one that has directly impacted my thinking and influenced the way I do things in class. The goal came from a girl already pegged as "gifted and talented." She enjoyed scholarly pursuits, read voraciously, wrote like a columnist and acted just right. I picked up her paper and read, "My goal is to build more."

The defensive me wondered why she had never asked for the building supplies, why she never came running at me through that window of opportunity I would always provide. Why hadn't she spoken up before this? I was quick to make it her fault.

The thinking me realized how predictable this situation was. For all the social reasons I understand, it would be rare for a girl to initiate such a request. Most of them wait to be offered, or request things of me in private or in their journal writing. Or worse, they just assumed the Legos weren't really something they could or should play with. Maybe they learned about Legos in kindergarten, or through TV ads, or at home. Or maybe they weren't interested in building gas stations.

Now we have two sets, one for the boys to use and one for the girls. I would have seen this as a ridiculous solution just a few years ago, but after reading the AAUW (American Association of University Women, 1992) report on "How Schools Short-Change Girls," it now seems like one small step in the direction of equity. If the girls wait for the boys to leave them some, it won't happen. If the girls wait for the boys to invite them to play, it won't happen. If I wait for the girls to ask me, it won't happen. If we all wait for divine inspiration to share the box of Legos it still won't happen. There is just too much to overcome. Too many messages, too many models and too many assumptions. I had to legislate the road to change.

I had to mandate equity. People who fought for Civil Rights would understand the thinking. You think you're going to wait for people to be fair? You have a long wait in store.

Sure, it's just Legos. But now the girls understand that all along they've had a right to play with them, that it's not up to the boys to "let them." The boys have learned a little about not being able to have all of everything, about having to give in and give up for all the right reasons. It's about equity.

I was furious when I heard that the Lego people were marketing new pink Legos in hopes of luring more girls and their parents into the lair. I was furious because once again I heard a male voice telling girls, "It's OK. I'm telling you, you can play with them too. Those are for you. We give you permission."

Parents, don't buy the pink ones. Girls, don't play with them, unless, of course the boys want them. But I know what boys have learned through life's hidden curriculum. They will turn them into the undesirable, inferior Legos within five minutes. They won't bother fighting over the pink ones. Those are the girls' Legos. Yuck.

This is not an attitude that comes from nowhere.
We condition our children to believe that girls play with dainty things and boys play with action toys.
Jack and Jill may have started up the hill together, but they quickly parted company when he became

The Jack on the Box

The next time you take a trip to your child's favorite toy store check out the pictures on the boxes on the shelves in the aisles in the stores that Jack built.

Pictures of boys are used to sell cars, computers, games and trains. Their faces grace boxes of glue-together jets, Legos, three-dimensional puzzles and chemistry sets. The pictures of girls will be found on the boxes containing dolls, make-up kits, stuffed animals and art projects.

Now this may not bother you nor may you think it inappropriate but it bothers the heck out of me. Times have changed but the way toys are sold has not.

Twenty years ago, when toys didn't require batteries, came with everything included and cost less than a new car some academicians conducted the only thorough study we could find of the pictures toy companies used to attract your child's attention. This is what they found. Keep in mind it was the '70s.

- On the covers of 800 toy boxes there were twice as many boys as girls.
- On boxes with pictures of cars, trucks and trains, only 2 percent had pictures of girls.
- On game boxes with boys and girls, chances were ten to one that girls were on the sidelines watching the boys play the game.

- On science and educational toys, boys outnumbered girls sixteen to one.
- On paint-by-number kits, girls outnumbered boys ten to one.

Now it's the '90s and women race cars and fly jets. They tackle just as hard on the peewee football team, win Nobel prizes in chemistry and design some of the toys kids want. But things haven't changed much on the pictures on the boxes on the shelves in the aisles of the stores that Jack built and Jill helped pay for. Legos may come in pink and there are female Power Rangers dressed in, what else, pink and yellow, but it's hard to call that progress.

What's good for the boy is good for the girl. The boxes containing Barbies, Little Mermaids, Baby-sitters and My Little Pony should not be the only toys where our daughters see pictures of people like themselves. Load up on the counter messages, Mom and fire off a few letters to the toy magnates. Level the playing field where you can.

Sure, boys will probably always prefer playing war to playing with curlers and girls will play dress up, fix up and paint by number but the pictures on the boxes on the shelves in the aisles in the stores that Jack built should give us all a break.

All we are saying is give Jill a chance. Ladies start your engines.

*Fire yourself up because when you're ready to face the perils in her feminine future,
you'll find Jack's toys are very different from Jill's. Your daughter is going to spend a lot of time*

CONQUERING & *Preening*

Anyone who has a child has been to one of the mega-toy stores which so inspired this piece. You've shared with me in the joys of shopping the mile-high aisles packed with junk your child has to have at one time or another in her life.

Since the conception of this book, I have found myself intrigued with toys and recreational products marketed for kids. When you begin to really see what you're looking at, it's scary. The subliminal messages blare through the packaging and promotion, and it pretty much comes down to boys conquer, girls preen.

From electronics to rubber action figures, males are the "doers." Boys conquer. Male children are targeted to idolize the doers, begin to see themselves as potential doers, and then beginning with toys, they become the doers. They conquer nature, they conquer the enemy, they conquer wild animals, they conquer great minds, they conquer matter in all its forms.

Girls preen. Girls comb and wash hair, cut hair, put on high heels and dresses, change hair, change shoes, change dresses, nurture,

baby-sit, accessorize, coordinate and after all that preening, they cook and clean.

Mothers, we are being set up. Corporate America must know that parents are way too tired, hurried and stressed out to wage a good argument of conscience. But my daughter is older now and I'm starting to get some sleep. I can see that I didn't even attempt to fight the good fight. She has every product ever made with a rainbow decal on it. She has lots of things to keep her "occupied."

That's it. She has been occupied. I lost the war before even hitting the delivery room. I lost my self-declared war on corporate gender manipulation. I admit it, but I was worn down. My daughter has fourteen Barbies she spends hours shampooing, blow drying and combing out. I even used to help her. She spends her weekends dressing and undressing, lining up and sorting all those barbies into believable clusters of friends and relations, all beautifully preened I might add. She has over eighty "Baby-sitter Club" books in her collection, a rubber baby doll she can bathe and cuddle and lots of stuffed animals.

Posed on the very end of her shelf as though contemplating suicide, stands her one X-man, Nightcrawler. "Jump" I yell as I pass by her room.

29

The biggest peril in constant preening is the manipulation of the psyche to believe that self-worth is tied to what Alice sees in the looking glass. Most of the time it starts right on top of your brain where it reigns.

STREAMIN' FLAXIN' WAXEN

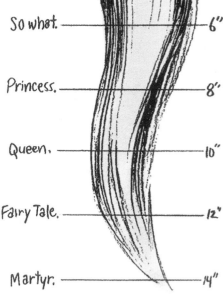

So what. ——— 6"

Princess. ——— 8"

Queen. ——— 10"

Fairy Tale. ——— 12"

Martyr. ——— 14"

My friend has a beautiful eleven-year-old daughter with long blonde hair. Hair like a goddess. Hair like a doll. Fairy-tale hair. Her self-image seems to have something to do with her untreated tresses and why wouldn't it? For years, every introduction was followed by, "You have such pretty hair!" or "Your hair is so long and beautiful!" One afternoon thinking out loud, her mother and I wondered if she would think herself as beautiful without it.

Maybe that all goes back to Eve. Maybe it's all her fault. Wild temptress, liquid locks. History is full of such trippy connections.

Call it the Lady Godiva syndrome. Same hair-do, same premise. Even when it was unapologetically fake, it worked. Marie Antoinette's towering coiffure helped change the course of history. For Rapunsel it meant freedom. Joan of Arc, shorn of locks, may be our only historical deviate, though she was burned at the stake. She cut her hair for more serious pursuits, something Eve, Godiva, the Cake Queen and even the famous prisoner would probably have understood.

But still we like little girls to have long hair. We braid it, brush it and endure the cries and whimpers when it's tangled. That is why we wondered what really happens when little girls get the courage to cut? Why? Would all long-haired beauties snip their locks earlier in life if they knew the freedom of the alternative, or if their best friend hadn't found the courage first? What would it take for an eleven-year-old girl to beg for a haircut?

The problem comes when the length of the pony tail is directly proportionate to the strength of the self-image. All little girls should be taught they are beautiful and that their worth has nothing to do with the length, color or cut of their hair.

So mothers beware. The brushing may be just the beginning. Your daughter may not want to ride naked on a horse, at least not until college, but she may begin to believe she is beautiful if and only if she looks like Cindy Crawford, or at least has her hair. Therein lies the danger. And that is pretty much the long and short of it.

No doubt she's going to believe some of the preening propaganda but there's a bigger challenge here. She's going to need courage to disdain, discard and debunk the real junk. Unless you plan on locking her away for eighteen years, start planning now. Take the time to unplug. We'll be:

BACK IN A MOMENT

Sometimes I am just plain embarrassed watching television with my ten-year-old daughter. As a good mother, I try to keep viewing time to a minimum, censor shows with violence or blatant sexual exploits and monitor what goes into her head the way I try to influence what goes into her mouth. This can be exhausting.

Seems to me we should all get a break during commercials, but now I find myself scrutinizing them even more than the regular programming. They're so compact, slick, and purposeful. So as she sits and watches, so do I, attempting to run intellectual interference with the steady bombardment of corporate crapola. Commercials and sports broadcasts are the worst and commercials in sports broadcasts are downright disgusting. Women are used as hooks. Hook the men into buying beer, after-shave, cereal, cars, underpants, overpants, ties, suits, razor blades and an image of women that is distorted.

So what do I tell my daughter as we watch the camera zoom in on a server's breasts as she bends over to take a food order? As we watch tight rear ends working out at the health club? How do I explain the Dallas cheerleaders? Why aren't there male cheerleaders in hot pants and boots? What do I tell her? Not much. I admonish myself for being such a lazy feminist. For some reason I'm having trouble talking to my daughter about breasts and butts and beer.

Sometimes when we watch commercials, I show no signs of processing any video input whatsoever. I sit catatonic, staring without comment at one piece after another, no pun intended. It's easier. Being enlightened creates so much work. I look over at my daughter. Yep. She's watching. She sees it. Now what? She keeps combing Barbie. I let that one go. It was just another beautiful actress selling pick-up trucks with a voice that would melt most 900 lines. Now comes the "lite" beer ad. Lots of breasts and butts and invitations. I have to say something. "What do you notice about the wardrobe they chose for the models in this commercial?" I ask. "Nothing Mom, why?" I cringe, turn off the TV and go get a bee...soda.

Sometimes it's very subtle. Passing for manners and proper etiquette, girls are taught all the sanctioned behavioral skills we so value as adults. Sure we want them to become part of a kinder, gentler world, but don't embrace all you hear. You may risk short-circuiting for the sake of:

Social Studies

My community newspaper is a nice alternative to the daily. It's filled with Youth Commission reports, articles on how police fight drunk driving and the local folks who have passed the 100-year mark. It's neighborly, one step above the shopper with an editorial page and a community calendar. I'm an avid fan, or was, until I saw this picture with the caption, "Social Studies." Clever editor.

The subtitle said "A row of young ladies practice sitting up straight, ankles crossed, hands folded neatly in laps. The occasion was an etiquette class, part of a mother-daughter tea at St. Roberts School."

St. Roberts School is a local, private Catholic school where girls and boys get an education that includes more than geography, math and music. There's catechism. But this picture was "girls only," and my first reaction was dismay. Rows of girls being taught to "sit up straight." There's nothing wrong with proper posture but I was saddened because I know little boys would never be so instructed, wouldn't do it if they were, and aren't even expected to learn. I wanted to scream through the newsprint to them and say "run in your Reeboks, put on your jeans, uncross your legs and let it rip."

Sure it's better for your bones to sit up straight and it's more practical to cross your legs at the ankle if you have on a skirt but there's something troubling about the photograph and the faces of the children.

We have a different set of rules for girls. It's part of learning to be courteous, something no generation has mastered since the '50s.

But I'd be willing to bet my five-button Levi's that fathers of the sons of St. Roberts don't go to teas, don't learn the same etiquette rules and probably need those skills more than girls.

Social studies is not a female-only subject, not any more than math is only for boys.

So sit up straight. Cross your legs at the ankles and fold your hands neatly in your lap. Then show your daughter how to question the status quo, start petition drives, write editorials and sit like she means business – in pants. Show her how to lean forward with nothing crossed. Teach her to put her hands in a pyramid when she speaks, fingers to fingers, thumb to thumb, and to ask the hard, probing, poignant questions. Then teach her how to gracefully leave when it gets to be a waste of time and a waste of mind. Now that's social studies.

33

Photo courtesy of CNI Shorewood Times

If manners matter so does empathy, something we rarely think of when we think of children. Take a pause when your daughter gives you one of those moments a Mom lives for, a split second of sensitivity combined with worldly wisdom. You'll hear a word, a phrase that soothes the psychological sunburn and massages:

MOM'S MANGLED EMOTIONS

I've been having lots of car problems lately. I drive an old car. I love it, I abuse it...kind of an automotive S&M thing, I guess. I've come to rely on it to the point where I don't even budget money for potential repairs or servicing.

A friend of mine convinced me that before our hard midwestern winter struck I ought to have the brakes checked. I didn't think the noise was that loud, but I agreed to do it and added a tune-up on top of that.

When I dropped off the car, I figured it would cost about a hundred bucks. I know you're laughing now, but that's how out of touch I had become.

During that workday, I found a pink phone message slip in my mailbox with the auto repair number written in the "please call" box. "Oh god," I thought, "this means money."

It's a good thing I was sitting when I made the return call because the repair was about $900 and I couldn't tell you everything they said needed attention. I went into shock after the word "dollars." They said it was not safe for me to drive anywhere, except possibly the ATM, without endangering my life and those of others. "Go ahead and fix it," I conceded, not knowing where the money would come from. I was improvising.

In a gesture possibly brought out by the holiday season, the people running the repair shop allowed me to pay in two installments. I knew that a lot of money divided by two still equalled a lot of money but thanked them profusely and went on my way with what I thought would be my like-new car. I didn't drive much that week, so at first I didn't realize that the car was running worse than before I took it in. In fact, it didn't run at all just after I applied the brake at any stop light, turn, stop sign or kid in the road. I had to start the engine each time my foot left the accelerator. It took me 15 minutes to get four blocks. This is not healthy for a Type A person.

I figured the car would heal itself overnight. Suffice it to say, it didn't. I called and took it in and they did what any overworked repair shop would do. They upped the idle. Pathetic in retrospect, but I bought it. I was in again two days later and a week after that. I had them change the thermostat as my car-guy friend suggested. That was another 80 bucks. I was writing hot checks and I knew it, but it didn't matter. I was losing my grasp. I needed a car, I needed to pay, I couldn't afford it. I chose not to care.

The day I picked up the car with the new thermostat, it died. So did the sense of humor that had carried me so gingerly through the past two weeks. I was on the edge. I was snapping at my daughter, eating bags of junk food and biting my nails like they were Lay's potato chips. I felt my backbone crumble. I was walking in the fetal position, if that's possible. I rolled the car into the drive, warning lights glowing on the dash, turned the key, went into the house and started to cry. I stood before my daughter, only ten, and sobbed in total frustration. I told her I was sorry for being so short with her lately, that I was broke and frustrated and explained the meaning of emotionally overwhelmed. She looked worried to see me this way and I worried myself. Luckily, I caught the repair person before closing time. She told me to bring the car in immediately and that they would fix it once and for all. I wasn't counting on that as I picked up my keys to leave. "I'll be right back," I told my daughter, wondering how I would even get home. "Do you want me to do anything for you while you're gone? Start dinner or something?" she asked. What a wonderful warm hand on my shoulder were those words. We both knew what she was saying. And she was right. Everything would be OK. Car or no car.

JUST WAIT 'TIL SHE TURNS THIRTEEN

Pre-teens through young adulthood

These are the years where you begin to discover the disturbing second decade, filled with pre-teen, teen and post-teen trauma. You'll hope to survive them with your sanity intact and at least some of your jewelry left in the drawer. If you have either, rejoice. If you have neither, relax. You're not alone. The shared burden has become the common condition of all moms. Completely perplexed by what passes for adolescence, you'll progress. First, all your clothes will disappear. Then, a few years later, she wouldn't be caught dead wearing anything of yours. Clothing consciousness begins with "the training bra." We want to know:

Why do they call them training bras, anyway?

When you go to buy your daughter's first bra and the clerk suggests a "training bra" don't you wonder to yourself, "What are we training her breasts to do?" Point the same direction and stand at attention? Both of those things come naturally until you're much older, then the law of gravity takes over.

Don't be shocked if your daughter says "forget it" to the training bra concept. The trendy alternative now, and usually long before it's really needed, is the short, midriff-baring-lycra fabric T-shirt, no clasps. It's a mini-version of the real training bra, the sports bra worn by women in training. Now they come with cartoon characters and colorful graphics in a clever new marketing approach. You'll pick out plain white and she'll say, "No, Mom, not that one. I want the one with the hearts on it."

A couple of years later, you'll know your daughter is growing up when she comes home from the mall with a new bra, bought with your money but without you. It's that same lycra-stretchy fabric but has a hook in the front and something like cups where you'd expect them to be. It costs more, looks more like the real thing and marks some sort of rite of passage when you're a teenager. Besides, all the other girls have them.

When the Victoria's Secret catalog arrives and disappears from the kitchen table before you get to see it, your daughter is grown. She's graduated.

She'll soon be asking if she can use your credit card because the 1-800 number is open 24 hours a day and there's this really cool all-satin, lightly padded creation called "Michelle" that would be perfect under this black strapless dress she ordered from your other catalog. You've lost her to the world of lingerie, underwired, laced up and plunging.

Now you know what the training was for. You, not your daughter's breasts. Training you to accept, in subtle stages of undergarments, her transition from little girl to woman.

If it stresses you out, think of it this way. Decades later she'll come home to visit, will be sitting at your kitchen table, leafing through your new Victoria's Secret catalog when she says to you, "Gee, I don't know what ever made me want to wear one of these things!"

It's amazing how smart your daughter turned out to be. She must have had good training.

For most moms, it's no longer a giant leap from bras to pierced ears. It was when I was a kid, but nowadays, infants have their lobes lanced and those a little older have so many perforations their ears look like fleshy Swiss cheese. Our daughters are going from crayons to perfume at earlier ages and moms are forced to stare adolescence square in the face even if they're not ready to:

CROSS THE
GREAT DIVIDE

Everyone's mother has said at one time or another, "You're too young for that." Mine was no exception. When I was twelve I wanted pierced ears, but I was too young, she said. "Wait until you're thirteen."

You're too young for that. What did that really mean? Were my lobes underdeveloped? Was my tissue immature? Did I have to be able to understand something complicated in order to wear them? What did those earrings signify to my mother? What was it? Was it something bigger than simply accessorizing?

It must have been. I had to wait the whole year. According to my mother, thirteen was that

magical age at which little girls could dip their toes into the waters of womanhood. But girls, beware. Along with the rite of passage comes the responsibility of proper fashion communication.

Flaunting your new-found womanhood and crossing from the cute zone into the dark, dank waters of the "tramp" zone can only lead to trouble. And before you know or realize it, all those around you have pegged you silently or even muttered "that little tramp."

That's what my mother called them. Tramps. And you know who they were. The "trashy" girls. Look back in your high school yearbooks. They jump out of the pages.

Earrings are but one item on the tramp test. For my friend, it wasn't the pierced ear, the size or even shape of the earring but the length of it. That threw her into a power trip she had trouble explaining and justifying not only to her daughter but to herself. Her struggle shows how deeply placed this bullet is, the conditioning that always nags at us just before fashion storms spring up.

She told me with great humility about her daughter and the first pair of earrings she wanted. The daughter chose long, dangly ones designed to complement black spaghetti straps or cocktail dress necklines, not Disney World T-shirts. "No," my friend ruled, "you're too young for those." When her precocious daughter pressed "Why, what's wrong with these, Mom?", my friend had to admit to having no real answer. No answer that made any sense, anyway. She just thought they looked trampy.

Then she made the grand admission. She looked her daughter square in the ears and said "I have no idea why I'm saying you can't buy those. If you want those, then we'll buy them." The tramp meter needle hit the danger zone and my friend, the mom, crossed the Great Divide between the prejudicial parentland of baseless myth and entered the valley of enlightenment. She had discovered there are few really good reasons to censor what your children wear.

Still, as the new millennium is poised to accept new standards, we couldn't resist ruminating over the question "Is trampy relative or can it be measured?" What is socially suspect now that it's the age of Kool-Aid green dyed hair, and nose, eyebrow, belly button and tongue rings?

Know that we're all still capable of raising eyebrows even now if we:

✗ have hair bigger than a doorway is wide.

✹ wear earrings in more than four body parts.

✗ wear five rings on one hand, two on one finger.

✗ wear bright red, glossy pink, or black lipstick and/or nail polish, unless you're more than seventy years old.

✹ wear black eye makeup.

✗ wear tight anything except jeans.

✗ brush blush more than four shades darker than your skin.

✹ wear eye shadow that sparkles.

✗ reveal cleavage.

✗ wear perfume strong enough to outsmell a Victoria's Secret.

✗ attract the attention of other women's husbands.

✹ wear an ankle bracelet under pantyhose.

✗ wear pantyhose under short shorts.

Even in the year 2000 a mother will have to have her standards.

*Just like the San Andreas fault, social standards are constantly shifting and each time
there is a fashion earthquake, you, Mom, are going to feel the aftershocks.
You may have thought the Peter Pan collar may be gone forever but don't bet on it.
What you thought was strictly the domain of the male of the species may end up in your daughter's closet.
In fact, some things seem to have a fashion half-life. Ever think you'd see the day when:*

YOUR MOMMA WEARS COMBAT BOOTS?

Your daughter comes home from a trip to the mall wearing her father's army combat boots. That's what they look like anyway and suddenly you feel old. You remember the time when women who wore combat boots and shoes named after doctors were ostracized and sexually suspect.

Things have changed, but it's hard to think of those shoes as anything but the kind worn by women who wanted to be men or were already in that man's army. Now fashion forecasters flaunt G.I. footgear on the feet of runway models from New York to Paris. Milan to Tokyo. Gaultier, Calvin, even Lagerfeld show army boots with lace, anklets and skirts so short they look like wide belts. What was military survival gear in one decade is overpriced hip gear the next.

It is "the style," or at least what "they" want us to buy — high fashion suitable for snow-clogged streets or college graduation. Now women can stretch out their toes, walk comfortably and run when they need to. But be ready for change because strappy stilettos are all the rage on the latest fashion page and your combat boots are soon to look like a trend gone bad.

Understand, everything is fashion fodder. When you embrace convention, surrender your wallet.

And understand it's all about change and never wearing what your mother would.

41

So we've come to the conclusion there are no more rules. America wears jeans to the opera and T-shirts to church. No shoes, no shirt, no service has become our fashion standard. There are no rules and we're becoming:

Fashionably INDIFFERENT

This little foray into fashion commentary started out as a laundry list of visually disruptive clothing combinations, styles and ideas that no woman would ever want to see her sartorially splendorous daughter wear. Simply said: advice.

Things such as:
- No woman should wear plaid pants – you just look silly.
- Avoid maternity clothes that make you look like the child you're having.
- Nothing plastic. No plastic shoes, no plastic boots, no plastic belts, nothing plastic.
- Avoid clothing with other people's names and phrases on them. Why be a walking billboard?
- Never wear white shoes before Memorial Day or after Labor Day.
- Never wear pearls before five or a brimmed hat after.

Really useful stuff such as:
- Appliqués shouldn't be worn by anyone over the age of nine.

- White socks mean serious business and are alternately trendy or silly looking off the tennis courts.
- Keep masking tape and staples handy. They work as well as needle and thread.
- Little girls never wear black unless it's the color of their shoes. Navy, especially velvet, is acceptable but never black.

Then a few things occurred to us in the process of reciting all of the above, handed down by our mothers and mother-like friends. Who cares?

Why should any woman, child or grownup spend one minute more worrying about what to wear?

We've been so conditioned that for centuries we've believed we had to follow someone else's arbitrary rules for what was socially, climatologically or visually acceptable. Who really needs to worry about whether polka dots (decades ago acceptable only on small children or old women) go with plaid? What difference does it make?

The answer is none. So we came up with a different set of rules to be totally ignored because none of this matters anyway. We just happen to like these rules better:

- If someone asks what you're going to wear to a social event, just say you're going to wear what makes you happy. Then forget about it and change the subject.
- Wear whatever makes you feel beautiful if that's what's important to you at the time. Wear whatever makes you feel comfortable if that's what you want. Wear whatever is warm, cool, or clean. It's your body, your decision. Nearly everything is acceptable anyway.
- Clothes are your body's touchable, washable, disposable artwork. If you want to wear someone else's name on your body, be a walking billboard. Contrary to popular thought, people who won't listen to what you have to say might read your T-shirt. Maybe not. Who cares?
- A ten-year-old girl doesn't need to worry about what she's wearing. She'll feel the pressure soon enough so don't question her judgment when she puts kelly green together with orange. It's not only acceptable now, it's trendy and called neon.
- "Rebellion" is fashion's first cousin, always more expensive than it should be and one scant season later, knocked off and found on K-Mart shelves but by then it won't be as much fun.
- If it's really ugly, your child will probably think it's really cool and your mother will think you're nuts for spending money on it. Just wear your ugliest with confidence. If you think we're wrong, remember hip-huggers or boxer shorts worn under cut-off jeans or white crew socks worn with Birkenstock sandals. See?
- Buy some stuff from second-hand clothing stores. It's much more fun, costs a lot less and you can find quality because folks who sell their clothes rather than just giving them away usually buy things worth hanging on to. They just don't because it's not fashionable.
- Wear whatever you like with confidence. If you're going to make what someone else considers a mistake, make it loud.

So these are our arbitrary rules and the ones we've decided to try and live by. We're going to wear what we like and hope we're never too young or too old to wear purple. But there is one thought that perhaps should be passed along.

At certain times, clothes do count. Think job interview. Even clothes without writing on them send a message, and often that message does matter because someone might not get to know the you you're so proud of if the outside you is screaming some sort of statement.

Clothes are superficial and in the long term won't make a difference in the conclusion someone reaches about your abilities, attitude or performance. But clothing is like a costume and you really should pay attention to the costume you're wearing if you're going to have to suffer the consequences of playing the part.

Provided you dress the part and get the job, promotion or assignment you want, play the part for a while until the real you can seep out without fear of overt rejection based on something as silly as clothing. Plan two weeks worth of wardrobes for the schoolroom, boardroom or sales room and then lighten up and forget about it.

Clothes do matter but they have too long kept women from concentrating on the really important stuff like finding work that matters or raising kids who know that life shouldn't be centered around your appearance.

Enjoy fashion for what it is— the world's most consistently changing industry designed to separate you from your retirement fund. And celebrate it when your ten-year-old really wants to wear her pajama bottoms with a black velvet jacket. She's showing real potential.

There will be a few years when your daughter will look to you for fashion advice. They won't last long. She'll grow up and you'll grow from omniscient confidant to out of touch, uncool landlord who crimps her hipness and flattens her fun. It's a natural part of the evolving life cycle and in a few short years you'll be back in your daughter's stylish good graces. Quite unexpectedly you may even experience a moment of bonding that transcends the generational distance. For me it was when:

My Mom ironed my hair.

Shoulder length and brown, parted down the middle, it was symbolic of the free-flowing '60s and just the beginning of my passage into a time most of the people of my parents' generation now regard as Armageddon.

It was a holdover from the English Music Invasion led by Marianne Faithful and dressed by Twiggy. It was cool, the coolest and was such a departure from the "flips" of the '50s that parents just shook their heads and thought we were probably all going to the devil because of it.

It wasn't easy to come by this perfectly straight mane, but no matter what your situation everyone tried to achieve "the look."

Jewish girls with envied curls did it. Dark-haired southern belles with big hair did it. Waspy blondes with too many overprocessed perms did it. Even those who had more in common with Marsha Brady than Joni Mitchell did it. We ironed our hair.

Actually, my mom ironed mine since trying to iron your own hair is physically impossible unless you're a contortionist. Those who had non-participatory moms would sleep with their hair wrapped around about eight orange juice cans with the tops and bottoms removed, securing everything with those long silver clips. They'd pray they wouldn't wake up with "ridges."

I tried cans a few times but they left me with sort of a pageboy look, definitely uncool and much too Captain and Tenille. It was Mom and the Proctor-Silex to the rescue, a three setting, cotton, wool and linen. She'd set up the old ironing board, wooden and creaky, in the basement rec room. She'd put the iron on the lowest setting, linen, I think it was, and comb my hair out onto the ironing board while I contorted my neck and body to get the most hair laid out. Then she'd cover it with a towel and press away, waiting for it to cool before she'd let me move. If it was straight enough, she'd section off the next piece and start again.

It was straightened that way for months. She didn't know why she was doing it any more than I really knew why I wanted her to, but she did it because she was my mom and it was important to me.

Fashion gave way to something else a few months later. I think it was the short, tightly curled and cropped look usually seen on revolutionaries. It wasn't really becoming on me so I stayed hidden under a beret of some sort most of the time. My mom stopped using the iron for anything except laundry.

A few years and several haircuts later there were family growing pains. The Vietnam War brought un-ironed hippie hair.

The counter-culture generation abandoned the American dream and my parents abandoned, for a while anyway, any hope that we'd all turn out OK. A couple of decades later when they realized their protesting offspring had created a new class of citizen labeled "the yuppie," everyone relaxed.

The irony of using the word irony and the orange concentrate beauty regimen hits me now thirty years later. My hair has been shorter, longer, blonder, darker, curlier, but never straighter.

It's almost 2000 and I find myself staring into the bathroom mirror after having coaxed my hair into a somewhat bubblish "do" with a little flip at the ends. Kind of a retro Mary Tyler Moore /That Girl look. A very trendy statement. Then it hit me. As I look at my straight hair I suddenly realize that a few years from now, a fashionable daughter is going to ask her slightly out of touch mother to set up an ironing board and plug in the iron because there's this really cool thing she wants to do to her hair. I plan on being around to tell her about her grandmother.

Of course, moms don't have a lock on sensitivity. Usually exasperated, Dad wants to be a cross between the father who knows best and a girl's best friend, but instead finds a tough tightrope strung across a deep chasm. Sometimes Dad stumbles onto a single experience that demystifies the female and lessens the confusion. That's good. But here will be lingering gender-based questions that cause Dad to wonder if

Father Really Knows Best

One of the men I work with has an outspoken, independent wife, one daughter, one son and a dog from the Humane Society. They have pursued the American dream and now have to deal with it.

I think of them categorically as social liberals and fiscal conservatives. She's a reporter for public television, he works for a commercial TV station that makes a lot of money. He seems to spend far more time at work than she does.

Talking with him about his children is always a learning experience for me because this is one interesting bunch. He's devoutly Catholic, teaching confirmation classes. She's a Lutheran who goes to meetings and drinks a lot of coffee. The dilemma of raising the children in one faith, not two, seems to have been settled in their household. I figured they're doing something right so I asked him about his child-rearing philosophies.

His kids are pre-teen so he's not totally freaked yet and the son does all the things accorded boys while the daughter does most of the things expected of girls. When I asked whether he worries about conditioning them to expect only certain things because of their gender, he admitted he worried about his daughter and whether she was going to be given all the opportunities his son was assured. He wonders is she missing opportunities now because she chooses to or because something different is expected?

The question may be centered around how much is learned behavior and how much is genetic. Sammi has no interest in cars and refused to show interest in them despite Dad's best efforts. Ricky has been fascinated by the sight, sound and touch of cold steel with wheels since he was given his first Matchbox car and heard his first faulty muffler.

Frank, the father, is convinced that Sammi's disinterest is genetic and not learned. But no scientist to date has discovered a "car-gene," floating around only in the bodies of boys. Sure, there are all sorts of impressive statistical and empirical data using all the right language to convince you children are born with inherent interests but there's no proof of anything.

Dad's not obsessing on these points, he's just conscientious and wondering how to accept the natural pre-programming and reject unnatural conditioning which is sure to creep into his daughter's life and get in her way. He hears Ricky say to Sammi, "you can't do that because you're a girl," and knows a lot of the world believes that bunk, too.

The best-seller lists are filled with genderflexing, genderspeaking and genderbending self-help guides comparing men and women to planets and life to a series of plays in a football game. It's all part of our lifespanning trek to find out what we are, what we've learned to become and what we really want to be without all the hype.

For Sammi it's the beginning of a life full of questions that speak to the heart of how we feel about our sons and daughters...our daughters who just want to know "Can girls play football?" and if they can, "How come there aren't any girl's teams?"

Sailing into this parental paradigm on the winds of change are females who grow up believing they too can crew on yachts and play polo. They've learned the boys' rules and they're beating them at their own games. Unless of course, they're told to:

Just aim for anything painted orange.

The gym teacher at the school in which I teach got an important call from his wife during one of his classes. I was in the office at the time and volunteered to cover for him while he took the phone.

I entered the sacred place, the gym, to discover two sets of children, one male set and one female. They appeared to be learning the fine art of shooting hoops. "Cool," I thought to myself, "the girls are being taught to play!" I went to watch the girls as the boys were clearly engaged in the competition they had created for themselves. The first girl walked up and half-heartedly hoisted the ball about a foot in the air. She laughed, covered her mouth and ran to the end of the line.

"Pitiful," I thought.

The next girl ran with a bit more enthusiasm and bounced one off the rim.

"Almost," I thought with some disappointment. This was shaken by an outburst of applause "What are you so happy about?" I called to the girls. "You missed. You don't get a point!" "Yes I do," the young player defended. "We don't have to make it through the hoop. Mr. H said all the girls have to do is hit anything painted orange!"

When the gym teacher came back after taking his call, I was almost sorry to see him return. All the students in the class were playing by the same rules. The girls were expected to make baskets, not be incapable of it. They were not praised for missing.

The girls knew I was angry and they saw me do nothing. He came back, I left and nothing changed. Nothing in his class, nothing

in his thinking, nothing in his consciousness. Nothing in their expectations of themselves. An ignored opportunity. Apparently I felt as intimidated by him as the girls did. I had the chance to score one for them and I didn't even throw the ball.

A lot of time has passed since this event but I want to take another shot at it.

Mr. H, I wish you would treat the females in your classes with more respect. I wish you would think about setting expectations high and demanding the best of all your students, including the girls. I wish you would think about what a humiliating message you sent to them and me that day. I wish you could remove the image of incompetence the boys may now have regarding their female classmates. I wish this insight would come to you, Mr. H, but I'm not getting my hopes up. I'm not convinced you've got what it takes. Doesn't feel too good to be told that, does it?

OK. Mental timeout. End of period. Score settled. Maybe this "one-upmanship" seems over the scrimmage line to you, but it's really more of the same old conditioning we think of as tradition and therefore somehow gender-sanctioned and appropriate. Forget it, we're not throwing in the towel that easily, but a couple of four-letter words made us feel like throwing

I listened once to a football coach talking about his high school team. How great the "**guys**" had done. How hard the "**men**" worked to pull off the win.

I thought about a coach for a "*girls*" basketball team because that is what we still called the all-female squad; "*the girls.*"

I tried to imagine a coach other than one at the college level saying how great the "*gals*" had done. How hard the "*women*" had worked to pull off the win.

It didn't sound right. At least it didn't sound familiar.

That's because "*girls*" has become such a pervasive term that we accept it in all sorts of applications (e.g., "So, you *girls* are writing a book, huh?").

Some of us even like being called "*girls*" because we think it makes us sound younger than we are and we believe that's a good thing. But as we have learned from other social justice movements, words can be powerful weapons in an unconscious war.

When I use the word "*girls*" I try to be sure I'm talking about *girls*: females before puberty. Those years between puberty and adulthood have me tripping all over my tongue in search of correctness. I hear myself referring to "young people," "young women" and "young adults." I can't get myself to refer to my young friends as "young ladies." It's a term tied to behavior and to me it sounds chastising and critical. Maybe it's the echoes of my mother and father, pointing their long parental, inquisitive fingers, asking questions like "Just where do you

think you're going?" or "Why are you getting in so late?" followed by the dreaded, "young lady?"

But "puberty plus" doesn't last long and girls quickly become women who have to deal with labels that define by the wrong terms. It's tough not to speak-think, just blurting out whatever pops into your cerebrum but it is the right thing to do.

Take care in your crusade, mothers. Being a girl is great if you're a girl. Being perceived and treated as a girl when you are a woman is not. Language is powerful. We can tell a lot about people by the words they chose. The next time he says, "So how's the old *girl*?" sing this out loud:

"Sticks and stones won't break our bones if words can help alert us."

49

There's so much between waking and times when she sleeps
even she starts resenting the schedule she keeps.
When we were the daughters our choices weren't as tough:
piano or Girl Scouts and one was enough.
But now it's alarms, planners and Filo-fax
and you're trying to keep up?
Forget it. Relax and

Get her a booking agent

First there's soccer on Mondays
   so much to do
Brownies on Tuesday
Wednesday jujitsu
Dance class on Thursday
Friday violin
By Saturday my interest
   in chauffeuring's wearing thin.

You're thinking it's the right thing
For the '90s child
But for a '90s parent it's ridiculous, it's wild
You're longing for a simple life
But simple it is not,
Because your neighbor just enrolled his little '90s snot
In fencing class, and Japanese, and art and diving, too
So rest when you've retired, the challenge is not through.

But bless the parent who supports
The child who draws the lines
When "I'm sick of the piano!" she with
   assertion whines.
You'll bristle first and then just smile
And say, "Are you sure, honey?"
Then grit your teeth and pray she is
Because you're out of money.

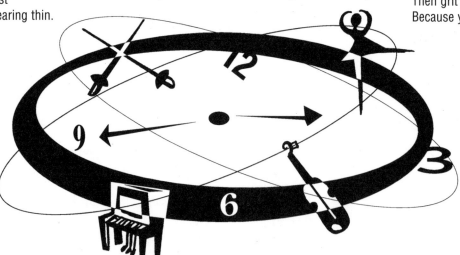

Money. Our chronic American condition is penny-pinched. Your daughter's financial future will not likely be much different.
Couple inflation with an historical propensity to underemploy women and you'll find troubling trends.
When women began to dominate the teaching profession, salaries dropped.
Some believe the same will happen when women, 42 percent of law school students, become practicing attorneys.
Even without that pessimistic overtone, the reality is scary enough so advise her now to:

Keep the change.

In 1994 women earned 72¢ for every $1.00 earned by a man. Female managers and/or administrators made about 90¢. The euphemism generally accepted is "Wage Gap."

The 72¢ figure increases about a penny a year, so by the year 2000 women will be making 78¢ for every dollar earned by a man.

If your daughter was 12 in 1994, she'll be 40 before she earns the $1.00 her male counterpart is earning now. The year will be 2021.

Start saving your pennies.

Money buys choice and choice buys independence. Men have long ruled the money-making world but women are learning that accounting is one part smarts and three parts creativity. We're making millions and learning how to spend it too. Buy a can of soup, money. Buy a house, the bank's money. Buy a plane ticket, plastic money. Cash flow in, out, debit, balance, tax, interest, income. Percentages, expenditures, decimals and decisions. It's a language our daughters need to speak. Face it. We've been financially cloistered. No more check kiting. No more promissory notes. The IOU is being called. We're subscribing to the Big-Street's Journal *and developing an affection for the color green. It's time she learned to play with more than:*

MONOPOLY
M·O·N·E·Y

Think about the game Monopoly. No one ever really teaches you all about it. You play it enough, you'll eventually get the hang of it. It's a rite of passage knowing how to calculate 10 percent of your income rather than pay the $75.00 luxury tax. You don't buy property right away, you wait until you're more Monopoly savvy and when you run out of money, you quit. Second mortgaging is so complicated. So who always won? The kids who knew the ins and outs of the game. The rest of us were just hoping to make it to the $200 handout as we limped around "GO". Go to your next PTA meeting and ask how many parents wish their children were more responsible about money. Hands would be up and waving like mad. We wish it, want it and come to expect it, but let's face it, most adults don't even do the responsible part well.

From the national debt to credit card bills at their limits, we haven't really been money mentors for the up and coming. It's fairly safe to say that no one really taught us money management until we were old enough to understand why it was important, which means we missed the most lucrative years of compound interest.

We've created a bad dream, American-style and not even the NASDAQ on a good day can make things better for our daughters.

By the year 2000 at 4 percent inflation (yeah, in your dreams), a 79¢ can of soup will cost 96¢. A $300,000 house will cost $364,995 and a $200 plane ticket will cost $243. Plan ahead are the watchwords for a child. Save those pennies.

Thinking money management while she's still in the crib might seem overreaching, but it's not. If only our parents had forced the issue of personal money management. By having us memorize the motto; "Start Early, Save Often."

Allowance. A word that strikes fear or guilt in the hearts of many parents because: do you or don't you, how much is too much, what isn't enough, should money be paid for doing chores?

These questions have simple answers.

To your child, there is no such thing as too much. No matter how much you decide, it's not enough. Allowances probably shouldn't be traded for doing chores. A smart girl will eventually link chores to work and remind you of Child Labor Laws. Media-psychologists believe chores are part of "family responsibility." Allowance is probably better if it's just a perk for being a kid.

But here's another idea. Consider an alternative to the weekly or monthly allowance. Try a yearly allowance. Take a blank checkbook (some banks will even give you books without account numbers) or make up one and have her write checks for the amounts she wants or needs. This system teaches the same skills as keeping a real checking account and keeps control where it belongs, with Mom and Dad.

She'll learn to keep the register, use a calculator, track her expenditures and deal with diminishing resources. Of course, this means that as a parent you have to have at least as much willpower as the child. When the money is gone, it's gone. No fair adding to the account or saying, "Oh, what's the harm. Just this once you can have a little more." That's called a loan and you know how those work.

If you give your daughter $5 a week in allowance that $260 all at one time looks like enough to buy a bike, fifteen computer games and a trip to Disney World. Reality will set in quickly, however, with one visit to the mall and one glance at the calendar.

Financial types call it "reality exchange." Normal moms and dads call it "reality check." Three shirts, four CDs, one pair of jeans and a book bag later, a year's allowance would be history. That's when your daughter will learn that money doesn't grow on trees or reproduce inside bank machines.

And that's your clue to introduce savings accounts. For each week or month that goes by without anything being debited from the checking account, give her a bonus amount to only be added to her bank savings account. Because of legalities, most banks or savings institutions will only let children open accounts with a co-signer. Do it together, don't do it for her. The first week or month make the amount nominal, say $5, calling it a savings bonus or earned interest. The second week or month nothing has been spent from the earned interest checkbook, increase the amount of the bonus by 5 or 10 percent. Do that for each allowance period. It doesn't sound like much and doesn't need to be, but she'll see it adding up.

As she and the savings grow, so will the commitment to the concept. With any luck, your percentages can outpace inflation and she'll start to like saving as much as spending.

Adults who manage money the same way, saving $150 a month, employing the 5-10 percent principal can end up with $60,000 after twenty years. That's enough to pay for three of her four years at Stanford. Maybe.

There are few things truer than this; "God bless the child who's got her own."

Repeat after me:
Start Early, Save Often."

Living by the money motto may mean more than just financial security for your fledgling. Flag down the latest flyer on the highway of human life and you'll find what social paleontologists are calling not the Fast Track, Mommy Track, or Laugh Track and certainly not the Back Track. Moms and Dads lead, follow or get out of the way because she's suited up, on autodrive and headed for:

The Daughter Track

Lee Heckt Harrison, an employment consultant, says her company surveyed more than 150 women entrepreneurs in the United States and Britain. She found the eldest or only daughters the most likely of that group to succeed. Over half (59 percent) were motivated to start their own businesses. Any ideas why? As the eldest daughter myself I don't find this a tricky question. We are used to having dominion. We are used to our ideas counting, having great self-confidence, and most important, having our own way! The study concludes the motivation for self-reliance comes from a primary belief in one's own abilities and a need to test them, coupled with the drive for professional autonomy. In short, we see ourselves as capable women and aren't afraid to go ahead and prove it. But we'd like to do it on our own, if you don't mind.

Barron's take note and make some space: According to the Small Business Administration (SBA) there are about 5 million women-owned businesses in this country right now and predictions are that women will own nearly 40 percent of small businesses by the year 2000. If you're one to cling to old paradigms, fasten your seatbelt, read this, and kiss 'em goodbye:

★ In 1990 women-owned businesses employed 11 million people, only 700,000 less than the Fortune 500.

★ In 1977, 2 million women-owned businesses had $25 billion in sales. By 1988 women owned 5 million businesses with revenues of $83 billion.

☆ From 1980 to 1988 the number of entrepreneurs increased 56 percent overall, but the number of female entrepreneurs grew 82 percent.

☆ In the same time period, revenues from entrepreneurs grew 56 percent overall, but revenues from female entrepreneurs grew *29 percent.*

What makes women so successful? It's ironic, but the same society that conditioned so many of us to be timid, empathetic, nurturing and collaborative peacemakers, is now the society looking for those qualities in its movers and shakers and corporate gurus.

So what qualities do women have that they like? We're cautious and although we generally play by other people's rules, we're learning to be risk takers. We are consensus builders, work better on teams and aren't afraid to hire someone more talented when there's a job to be done. After years of raising families and micro-managing households, it seems women have tapped their natural leadership styles (both cultivated and biologically based) to fit into the "progressive management model forward thinking businesses are widely endorsing." That's an observation made in the concrete canyons of Wall Street by the *Journal* and translated here to mean, what works in business these days are managers who can think like Mom, keep cool like Mom, schedule, cajole and support like Mom.

Lest we leave you with the idea that it's only the birth canal leading directly to the "Daughter Track," read on. Women are highly suited to taking the social skills we have not only as mothers, but as daughters, wives, friends and colleagues, and parlaying those into something bigger, better and almost always more lucrative, often without even leaving the house. Economic guru Peter Drucker says there is a "new breed of entrepreneur," a person who looks at identifying a social cause, creates an opportunity and turns it into a profit.

Want examples? How about Mary Kay, Jenny Craig and Martha Stewart! Count your change before you laugh.

Some estimates claim that in this country right now there are more than 40 million telecommuters or salaried employees who split the work week between home and office. With 36 percent of the labor force home-based today, by the year 2000 estimates are it will be well over half. Maybe some nice memory expansion or a 28,800 baud modem for her graduation?

Take the social trends and economic forces in today's world and combine them with the character traits common in our daughters and stand back. The potential is like magma. The result will be volcanic. The track may be paved with igneous rock.

It's certainly something to think about as you're watching your daughter grow. When your five-year-old wants to start a lemonade stand out on the sidewalk or buy her own lawnmower and take on the neighborhood, encourage her to venture out into the muck and mud. And don't you worry about the tracks.

*With financial security and the investment she's made in self-assurance, your daughter is off to meet the Wizard.
She may find the Emerald City and head straight for the office with the big, spinning leather chair.
The Chairman of the Board may not know it now, but his future leader may be setting up shop in your backyard.
Prepare her early so the letters that begin "Dear Mom" end with:*

Your Daughter the CEO

"We want workers who can make good decisions, be team players, be listeners as well as talkers, be consensus builders." Blah blah blah. What business wants, what corporate America wants, just may be your daughter. The qualities they are describing need not be drilled into tomorrow's workers. Girls already have them. Sit and watch a group at play and you'll see what we mean.

Girls bring their own particular strengths to the genealogical table and while all are valuable in childhood they are highly marketable and profitable for many in adulthood. All apply to girl-children but if there are two or more siblings in the room, none apply.

Girls are often good listeners as well as good talkers. The person who negotiated the Middle East Peace Accord's agreement between Yassar Arafat and Yitsak Rabin was a Scandinavian woman who listened to both men and then talked them into listening to each other. Simple technique; listen, talk, listen, talk.

Girls are givers as well as takers. They may sometimes have difficulty sharing because they're kids, but girls won't fight over toys as much as boys. They'll share the fun and most often come to the conclusion they need to on their own.

Girls will negotiate for what they want. They'll trade you a clean room for a night of their favorite TV shows but they'll do it straightforwardly. Girls can laugh with each other without laughing at each other.

They don't have to make each other uncomfortable for the sake of humor. The scales are almost tipped, in that most self-deprecating humor comes from female comics. We ought to work on this part.

Girls will compete against each other for years and still end up friends. Chris Evert and Martina Navratilova proved it.

Girls will argue with each other one day and forget about it the next. They know they need each other's support.

Girls will help their best friends do whatever needs doing in order to get somewhere. Picture Lucy and Ethel stuffing their faces with candy from the conveyor belt on the factory production line.

Girls rarely hit, punch and shove unless there's a boy involved. Excluding trendy kick boxing for defense, women don't crawl into a boxing ring to batter each other's brains out under the guise of sport. This gentleness hasn't survived the boardroom. Yet.

Girls rarely order each other around. They'll discuss for hours what to do, where to go, what to play, how to do something. There's a lot of "you want to..." in their conversations instead of "we're going to?..." This of course is not always a positive thing if you're an adult trying to pick a restaurant for dinner.

Girls will get past the difficulties. Ask Hillary Rodham Clinton and Kathleen Gingrich, Newt's mom. The whole "bitch" flap was little more than fodder for the tabloids but Kathleen ended up with tea and a tour of the White House.

Girls will volunteer their feelings sooner than opinions. They know feelings are OK but with opinions they're not so sure.

And that's when the caution flag should drop. It's the beginning of the age, the time, the moment when girls will start to have lower expectations for themselves than will boys. They'll blame themselves when they fail and think it's luck when they succeed. Those are the warning signs that their psyches are getting bent and the seeds of insecurity are growing.

So be the one to call the board meetings every now and then to review those five-year projections. Prepare your daughter intellectually and emotionally to give her all and accept her due. Send her out into the world meaning business, with confidence and style. Forget the big leather chair. She won't be sitting.

She may instead be jetting around the globe from her "virtual" office better described as a laptop computer and a world pager with voice mail plugged into her cellular phone. If she isn't already online and she's over the age of six, what are you waiting for? She needs to be hopping the World Wide Web and hanging her baseball cap on a new horizon. She needs to go to Las Vegas where the sign is out:

help wanted

Comdex.

One word that sounds like an acronym, says absolutely nothing but means Mecca to computer lovers. It's the annual electronics show in Las Vegas, where acres of hyped-space become cyberspace. Every year the glitz that is Sin City gives way to hundreds of thousands of interfacing Interneters.

The sociological challenge of the convention was not to snap up the latest in virtual reality but simply to find the women who in reality were virtually nonexistent.

Oh yes, there were some women there. They were posing beside displays of the latest in software, the newest in

hardrives or the hottest in game toys for game boys. They were pointing and smiling, demonstrating and coaxing. They were part of the hook and dressed as one can only in Vegas.

There were a few super model superstars peddling their own software for exercising on CD-ROM and a few more in the pornographic section. That was so offensive it was later moved out of the convention altogether, housed in another hotel across "The Strip" and called Adult-Dex. It was organized by a woman who said she believes everyone should have a choice. Viva Las Vegas! What a gig! If you don't count the peddlers, pushers and pretty girls designed to "face" the products, there were by most accounts fewer than 20,000 women in attendance or fewer than 10 percent of the folks riding the wave of the future.

If women are going to surf the Internet with the technoliteracy of their male counterparts, then it's time to grab the motherboard and hit the beach. Trade in the bikinis. Numbers from the Bureau of Labor Statistics show two of the best paying job categories for women are computer science and engineering in applied science and technology fields. Better news yet is that the wage gap for women computer scientists is the narrowest. Women make 89 percent of what their male counterparts make and while that may not sing R-E-S-P-E-C-T through your radio, it's better than the overall average of 72-74 cents on the dollar.

By the year 2000 this country will need almost 400,000 new systems analysts and around 300,000 computer programmers. The people who have those skills will be hotly pursued and well-paid.

The world doesn't run anymore without Windows, Quicken and Claris and it's going to be more of the same, not less. Women should be at the keyboards calling the shots, not waiting on the guys drinking them.

Computers are the modern-day catapults to equal opportunity and the electronic touchstones to success and independence. They don't know if you're in boxers or WonderBras and don't care! Everyone is on a level playing field where the boundaries are only the limits of the brain.

Some young girls probably already know that. If you ask just about any six-year-old, they'll tell you they love computer class where they write, draw, do their math problems and play, but it is more than a matter of just being booted up and online. It's a lifeline and it gives little girls a power and strength unequaled by any other learning tool. The sky-high prices of yesterday have fallen faster than hemlines during a recession so find a way to afford the keyboard, monitor, CPU and CD-ROM. Powerpack your daughter's way into the modern work world.

Get ready—your daughter may have to modem-fax your birthday greeting in a few years because she'll be expo-hopping, checking out the latest tools on the techno-track from places like Comdex in Las Vegas. Get her going now and she won't be the one wearing Spandex and a smile.

JUST THE FAX, MA'AM.

PHONE VOICE MAIL MESSENGER INTERNET FAX LACK THE **HUMAN** SOUNDS AND SCROLL

these are
the future.
interpersonal
communication
interfacing through
cyberspace may be
your daughter's
only way of
staying in touch.

TECH TALK.
BUT THE WORDS WILL
KEEP THEIR MEANINGS.
BEFRIEND TECHNOLOGY,
KNOWING THAT ITS
SHARP SOUNDS
AND HARD EDGES
ARE CAPABLE OF
DELIVERING THE
SOFTEST OF THOUGHTS.

Return your daughter's kindness with some of your own. Forget the flowers, blouses and bubblebath. Give her a gift that will keep on giving. Give her a power gift. Something even better than diamonds. Because even though a ring on the hand may be quite sentimental,

MUTUALS ARE A GIRL'S BEST FRIEND

How about a portfolio
filled with stocks and mutual funds from multi-national corporations
investing in fast growing, innovative communication technology companies interested
in growth cyclicals and evergreen endeavors complementing
the sociological sensitivity of a little girl

Throw in :

a fax machine
a calculator
a 1,000 piece 3-dimensional puzzle
a chess board
a copy of the "RISK" game
on CD-ROM

or maybe

flying lessons
a tool box
batteries
magnets
a microscope
a computer
an electronic date book and planner
a bat
a fishing pole

Or how about a power gift?

The sole remote control?

Mom's Invisible Umbilical

If you learn now what I learned the hard way

You can buy her all the right electronic gizmos. You can help her find the smart, directed and accomplished woman ready to burst from inside her girl's body. You can help her through the life-questions that have no clear answers. But there is one thing you cannot do. You cannot prepare her for her first visit to a gynecologist. It defies description. It is a rite of passage through unknown territory dark with fear. There is no secret. It's best just to tell her:

You never get used to it.

The first time I went for a pelvic, thank goodness my mom had the instinct to just drop me off at the office door. She knew. She knew there are some things a person just has to do alone. She spared me from having to make conversation in the waiting room and she knew I knew she knew everything that went on in that room and that I was not the kind of person to want to discuss any of it. She put just enough distance between us so I could shake the whole experience off as I walked outside to find her waiting for me in the car. Thanks, Mom. Had she been with me we would have had to talk more directly and this always embarrassed me for some reason. Instead, I told her about the receptionist's hairstyle and color du jour, an article I read in an old waiting room magazine and hashed over dinner possibilities with her. Distance can be such a gift.

 We didn't talk about bodily functions, changes or maintenance when I was growing up.

We were intellectuals. We didn't acknowledge a lot of what the body did or needed. We read. We read pamphlets, encyclopedias, medical books, and AMA magazines. My dad was a physician and my mom was a nurse. Neither of them had the nerve to explain a gynecological exam. Clearly, they knew too much.

 I went to our family doctor. That was a mistake. There was something that gave me the creeps when the same guy who took care of my grandmother was giving me a gynecological exam. To make things worse, he talked about what a nice person my mother was and made me promise to send her his regards. Ugh. All I could think about was that in a few minutes I would probably be, at the least, partially naked.

Anyway, I'm pretty sure we talked first. Foreplay to make us comfortable with the whole thing. He shook my hand, I answered questions like, "When did you have your last period?" I never kept track of that except later in life when I was trying to get pregnant. To this day, when asked that, I just make up an answer. That is not helpful.

After we chatted, I was sent off with a young woman who escorted me to the exam room where I was instructed to take off all my clothes and put on some tissue wrap. She said this so nonchalantly as though it were no big deal. How could she tell me this without bursting out laughing? I didn't remember whether she said it opened in front or opened in back, so I wrapped one side over the other in front and belted it like my terry cloth bathrobe. I was ready for *Mirabella*. I was looking pretty good for someone wrapped in paper, except for the burgundy knee socks. I wasn't sure about those. Do I leave those on? Take 'em off? Why couldn't I leave them on–what difference could they possibly make? Why would I need my socks off? I was nervous, but not so much that I didn't know I looked pretty funny buck-naked, except for tissue paper and knee socks. I was starting to panic.

So I slid my kneesocks down to my ankles in some sort of desperate, compromising move. They looked like two wool innertubes, all baggy and bunched. "That looks ridiculous," I thought, and pulled them back up. I was clearly starting to lose my senses. It had been fifteen minutes now. I wasn't used to sitting this long fully clothed, much less naked except for the knee socks, which now in this stark white room on my pale white skin seemed to be just screaming out.

I sat and stared for that first fifteen minutes. Stared at the instruments, stared at the curtains, stared out the window and wondered if the people in the high rise down the block were laughing their heads off at my burgundy socks through their binoculars. I decided to do what every intellectual does when nervous. Read. Just as I was peeling myself off the roll of paper at the end of the exam table to rifle through some bad magazines, I heard two rapid knocks as the door opened. He didn't even consider leaving time enough for me to say, "Come in."

What happens next is a rite of passage into womanhood. A truly personal experience best left to discuss with a rowdy group of your closest friends over bad margaritas somewhere. We all go through it.

We should and have to. It's embarrassing, at best, and humiliating at worst. We've all known both. Next time you find yourself waiting on a roll of paper in an exam room listening to MUZAK, think about all the women you know, lined up in turquoise tissue, naked as jay birds with only knees socks on. Picture your attorney, Supreme Court justices, bosses, first ladies and the incoming gynecologist all goosebumped, kneesocked and waiting for you. You can laugh about it, but there's just no getting used to it.

Sometimes your best advice is going to be ignored. Don't take it personally and don't consider it a rejection of your mothering skills. Your daughter is finding her way, exploring her options and taking control. There will be that fated moment however when all your fears come in the form of a testosterone-packed, six-foot college dropout with three earrings and dirty fingernails. It's OK. Resist the temptation to trash him and believe she'll eventually see for herself what it took you years to learn. In lieu of advice, just give her this list so she knows to:

AVOID DATING MEN WHO:

Wear baseball caps adapted to hold two cans of beer and rubber tubing that siphons it into their mouths. Go to their mothers every Sunday because they say they "have to." Were high-school football quarterbacks They probably peaked twenty years ago. Stop in without calling. Spit and/or scratch a lot. Refer to you as "Babe" or "Sweetie." Don't introduce you to people when you're standing right next to them. Point at  Abstract Expressionist art and mumble "I could do that." Refer to male ballet dancers as "girly boys." Have names for their penises. Wear their initials on their rings, shirt pockets and cuffs, all at the same time. Have more than two tattoos, any one of which involves a serpent. Wear belt buckles bigger than paper plates. Call you more than six times in a single day. Refer to their cars, boats, snowmobiles and motorcycles as "she." Borrow money from you. Interrupt you with their business while you're on the phone doing your own. Say "I'm separated" when you ask if they're married. Phone or fax you without identifying themselves. Say "Hi, Honey" when you're not their honey. Have their secretaries order flowers for you. Have regular, standing dates for their manicures. Count the number of cookies you eat. Count the number of anything you do. Can't cook anything that doesn't come in a box or out of a can. Signal their arrival by honking the horn and after dropping you off pull away before you get in your front door. Don't flush. Have framed magazine photos of Arnold or Rush. Won't let you drive his car. Wouldn't consider having a male secretary. Don't own any hardcover books.

There is one moment that convinces moms their daughters have roared onto the highway of independence and are shifting into overdrive. The first driver's license eventually gives way to the need for a first car and that means freedom. Although we have to admit that a few of us never master parallel parking, some of our daughters may end up driving Indy cars. Whatever her auto-acuity, put the pedal to the metal, Mom, and help her prepare to deal with her first car salesperson. She's about to experience:

Four-Wheeled Freedom

First things first. Help her understand all that glitters is not perfection. "Oh, it's so pretty" is not a good reason for buying a car. Help her educate herself before she steps onto the sales lot asphalt. Buy *Consumer Reports* to prepare her. Learn something about engines, maintenance and safety. Find out about carburetors and timing belts and then pass it along. If you don't, she'll be like carrion in the dealership desert and the smiling vultures will circle.

When she's ready to go shopping, go with her. Walk in purposefully, with the attitude that the car is worth half of what they are charging. As a general rule of thumb that's pretty close anyway. Help her understand she shouldn't even consider paying what they ask. If you immediately feel pressured, leave. They'll run out after you.

Suggest to your daughter that if there are no female salespeople at the dealership you should shop elsewhere. It's a matter of negotiating on even turf but if both of you are lousy at negotiating, don't let this be your training ground. A proud mom should never be too proud to help her daughter become the best negotiator she can and sometimes that means watching someone else do it well. Take with you someone who is unemotional, removed from the transaction and then watch her/him work. If the person you choose is male and the salesperson speaks only to him, request another salesperson—specifically a woman. You can think of yourselves as apprentices. Learn to keep quiet no matter how much she wants the car. When she takes her dreamboat out for a test drive, help her decide what she's willing to pay. If you don't know much about cars yourself, refrain from offering the banalities. "It smells so new and it rides real nice" is not going to help and makes the whole process much too personal.

When she's found the little red number with the CD player and all-weather radials and insists it's the only car she wants, you've got the caution flag. If it's used, have her request the car be checked over by a mechanic and ask for the name and phone number of the previous owner. If they won't give it to her, walk. If it's brand new, ask for all the little junk. You know, the coffee cup, the floormats, the deodorizer, the window tint, a radio, a full tank of gas when you leave, etc. She'll never find them quite as accommodating as before the sale is made.

If the name of the dealership has the word "Wreck" in it, don't bother stopping.

She's now free. She'll drive her traveling time capsule on Michelins, stereo blaring and top down, right out of your daily life and into some faraway sunset. You need to arm her with enough knowledge to avoid a major crash and supply her with enough humor to get out of the way of swerving sociopaths. Flip on the signal and move over; it's time for some serious and not so serious:

Thoughts on driving

- Learn to drive. Learn to drive a stick. Learn to drive a stick on the freeway. Learn to drive a stick in the mountains. Let no terrain go unexplored.

- When a driver tailgates on the freeway, slow down, adjust the rear view mirror and smile when he throws you a dirty look.

- If you're going to yell and scream at other motorists, be sure you do it only when the windows are up.

- If you're Type A, it's a good practice for you to stay in the right lane and not pass, no matter how much you want to. Builds character.

- Change a tire when you don't need to. Practice in your driveway on a nice warm day. That way if you can't get some Good Samaritan to help you on a cold, dark night in December, you can always do it yourself. Knowledge is power. Knowledge that you have knowledge is reassuring.

- Whenever you get gas check all the fluids. If an idiot light goes on, stop the car. Even if it turns out you just needed windshield wiper fluid, it's better to be safe than humiliated by a loved one later on.

- When you buy your first car get power everything. It gives you another kind of reign over your environment.

- Even if you live in a warm climate learn how to drive in snow and on ice. It gives others one less person to scream at when the first snowfall hits.

- There is a power seating echelon in automobiles. Know that riding in the back denies you any automotive control.

- Take turns driving on dates. Find out his enlightenment level. When you double date, tell both males to sit in the back. Listen and observe.

- Learn to read maps and give directions. Try not to refer to left and right as "this way" and "that way."

- Have and learn how to use booster cables. If other people can figure it out, you can too.

Watching her drive away in her first car will be a bittersweet moment. Signing the lease on her first apartment will strike fear in the heart of even the calmest, most collected mother. It means no more monitoring her comings and goings. No more monitoring the comings and goings of others. It's the final warning shot fired over the heads of parents who are about to do battle with young adulthood. When the smoke clears and the assault on your psyche is over, you'll actually be proud that she's:

On Her Own

If you're clever you will have sent her off with a carton of Spackle. She'll have a box full of tools because you've been giving them to her as gifts since she was five. She knows screwing in screws with a butter knife and hammering with a stapler works but isn't time efficient.

She may have a nomad mentality. That's OK.. Keeping acquisitions to a bare minimum means less to move when it turns out a high school rock band lives down the hall. She may know what you never considered; living as though you might have to pack up and move at any moment has its advantages. You'll share one of those memorable motherly moments if you check out the apartment with her, camping out in the hallways for a few hours at dinner time. You'll both find out where the babies and loud sound systems are located.

Mom, she's going to have roommates and get used to the fact that one or more of them may be of the opposite sex. Do not worry. The biggest problems she'll have are making sure they don't eat her food in the refrigerator, do their fair share of the cleaning (remind her the old chore chart works) and remember to contribute to the rent on time.

You've taught her well. She knows to never say "Oh, that's OK!" to the manager because nothing will ever get fixed. She knows to put on the downstairs mailbox a name like Bruno. She knows to never take a first date home because he may turn out to be wacko and it's better if he doesn't know where she lives. She knows to never just buzz people in, but to go to the lobby and check them out. She understands that pepper spray is no substitute for good planning and quick thinking. She won't say "I'm not home now" on her answering machine. Her message will say "I'm cleaning my gun" or "I'm feeding the pit bull." You've done your job. She's going to be fine and no matter how she lives, her life is not going to be ruined if she doesn't make the bed.

Those were easy words of advice. These will be tougher. When the spiral of interpersonal relationships recoils like an out-of-control Slinky, sometimes there are no words of solace that will ease your daughter's trauma. The best you can hope for is that when the web of human interaction gets tangled, she'll remember some of your:

Home-Grown Homilies

"A relationship is over only when both people are dead." We heard that on the TV show "Sisters." If you have a sister or an ex-husband you know it's true. Your daughter needs to know it, too.

"Avoid love sick love songs where women are victims." That means when you buy her music, you'll have to stay away from the country and heavy metal sections.

"Love shouldn't hurt. If it does, it isn't." Oprah said it. She's right. Pass it along.

"Yes, I know he's the only one." Chances are there are thousands of only ones out there. Give some of them a chance.

"You are not incomplete if you are not half of a couple. You are not complete just because you are." Enough said.

"Of course marriage takes work. Any relationship takes work." But be sure to add that when it begins to feel like work, she should take a vacation.

"We are lucky to live our lives and at the end be able to count on one hand our true friends." She needs to know it's good to live a two-fisted life.

If she remembers the above she'll do fine, at least until she runs into a relationship red flag. Sometimes it's difficult to recognize an ending. She needs to listen carefully to what the love of her life says. These all mean "it's over."

"There will be others, you know."
"This has been special."
"I have never loved anyone like this before."
"It's always been fun; I'll never regret one day of it."
"I'll miss the warmth."
"I don't think we should kiss."
"I need to go away for a while."
"I'll see you again sometime."
"I'll never forget you."
"I'm not seeing someone else."
"I just need time to think."
"I could be back before you know it."
"I hope we can still be friends."
"You deserve someone better."
– and our personal favorite–
"No, it's not you. It's me."

71

There is no way to ensure that your daughter's eventual choice of a permanent life partner is going to be successful.
There isn't a checklist for "Mr. Right," no fill-in-the-blank personality quiz ripped out of a women's magazine that will work.
Despite the trial-and-error nature of the way we choose the person with whom we will endeavor to stay attached,
we remain undaunted by the challenge and suggest you offer your daughter these observations. Consider this sort of a thumbnail sketch of:

The **Perfect** Partner

He's capable of sharing time, space and responsibility. Keep careful note of how much he contributes to the general maintenance of the home. If he says things like "where do you keep the mop?" tell him "in the backyard" and then lock the door while he's out looking for it.

He, when speaking to male friends about caring for children, refers to it as "playing with the kids." If he calls it "baby-sitting" or "keeping the kids," end it.

He loves his mother, visits her often but never takes his laundry for her to wash. If he does, dump him. If he lives with her and she's perfectly healthy, run.

He clears his own dishes, calls in sick for himself, fusses over coffee preparation, lets the answering machine get the phone even when he's home, nags you about picking up after yourself, and sorts dirty clothes by color and texture. If you managed to stumble across someone who does all of the above, propose.

LIFTS UP TO 250 LBS.

AMPLE STORAGE SPACE

GOOD TEETH.

CAN REACH OBJECTS ON TOP SHELF.

MR. WONDERFUL · 6'2"

He believes that a woman should keep her own name upon marrying, or should hyphenate using both. Then he volunteers to do the same.

He thinks keeping separate saving accounts is a good idea and believes couples should pay bills together.

He would never think of using the term "my old lady" or "the little woman." If he does, any woman who hooks up with him has a lot of work to do. It might be fun to take a cruise instead.

Our final thoughts on men who have the potential to be perfect partners:

- Men who do not have women friends probably don't know how to be one.

- Men who do not have male friends probably don't want the competition.

- Men who have women friends shouldn't be expected to give them up.

- Men who have male friends won't even consider it.

Our preceding thumbnail sketch would have helped at least one woman who could have saved herself a lot of grief had she applied our criteria. Despite the fact that she was a somewhat conservative social revolutionary, your daughter probably won't read about her in history class, won't find a T-shirt with her likeness in the local bookstore, and won't know the courage it took to practice what she preached by:

STONE WALLING

In 1855 Lucy Stone kept her name when she married Henry Blackwell. Her social strata shook right down to the pre-Cambrian shield. Such things were just not done and were not considered ladylike behavior. Lucy had some revolutionary ideas about equality but she had a lot to learn about Massachusetts where keeping your own name meant risking imprisonment.

Now more than a century later, the Lucy Stones of the state are off the hook and without threat of manacles because of monikers.

Women in Sweden have a different story to tell. In the 1980s their Parliament passed a law saying women and men may choose to be called by their spouse's name. That's men and women and the operative word is choose. That means when Bridgett Youngquist marries Jan Lindquist she has options and can call herself Bridget Younguist or Bridgett Lindquist and Jan can do the same. He can become a Jan Youngquist.

If Bridgett and Jan decided to have children, the girl-child could be called Youngquist or Lindquist and the boy-child Lindquist or Youngquist or both could decide to hyphenate their names and become a Youngquist-Lindquist or a Lindquist-Younquist or maybe one of each. No kidding, and it explains the length of the Swedish phone books.

If Bridgett and Jan couldn't decide what surname to give the newborn, the state, just as Massachusetts did a century earlier, steps into the name game. After three months of no name, the child is given the mother's surname. End of confusion, end of debate.

Lucy Stone was a revolutionary of the first degree and had the right idea. If your daughter marries and feels obligated to change her last name remind her that cars in Europe keep their plates no matter how many owners. And that is how the name game should be played.

The name game continues more than a hundred years later with people still referring to the name women are given at birth as a "maiden name." It's time for your daughter's generation to throw off the mired-in-the-19th century terminology and create a few new traditions. Say good-bye to that which signifies ownership and to:

The Ring That Binds

Watching a newly engaged woman is sort of like watching the coronation of a Queen. There's a lot of proffering of the left hand with the shiny new bauble and always a lot of "ohhs...and ahhs!" coming from the women who gather around. That gentle gesticulation sets the tone for the group and a somewhat regal atmosphere permeates, the only deviation being that squealing noise men recognize at forty paces, their signal to evacuate. It's something only women share or at least I find it hard to imagine men saying "Hey, Bob, let me see your new wedding ring. Wow, that must have cost a fortune."

I had forgotten about all that hullabaloo that goes with the formal request of someone's hand in marriage until a couple of women I work with were asked, accepted and set out to co-habitate. One was unabashedly forthright with her intent. "Children," she said. She wanted children. The other said no children, never. A dog, maybe.

Both insisted nothing else in their lives was going to change. They were going to keep the same friends, same apartments, same goals in life and separate checking accounts.

Having been a veteran of a long-standing marriage, I nearly laughed out loud at that last part. You may go in with all these grandiose ideas of equality with equanimity, parity with your partner and fervor in your lovemaking but pretty soon you'll realize you're just like everyone else and so is he. You both get too tired for anything except the late news, your checking account is more mangled than managed and now there's someone else in the house who thinks it's OK to go into your wallet.

It's a strange thing, marriage, and trying to explain to your daughter that it can be wonderful skirts some of the main issues that moms are bound by some unspoken code to pass along. So here's a quick reality reference to be snipped out and handed over to the next woman who swears nothing will change.

- First rule, everything changes. You begin to assume washing the car is his job and he thinks doing the laundry is yours. Break that notion early on.

- Hide money. It's the only way to stay ahead. Get yourself an old coffee can, a pair of slippers, or a high-yielding fund with a portfolio full of low p/e small stocks. Stash what you can and never use it for household expenses. It's yours and you're entitled to it.

- Encourage him to go out Friday night with his buds, play Saturday morning soccer and watch football all day on Sunday if that's what he likes. You're going to spend the rest of your life with this guy so there's plenty of time to go around. Take your space by giving him his.

- He used to always look great. Pulled together and coordinated. Now it's sweat pants and flannel shirts. Even if you don't like his style, never nag him about what he's wearing. You hated it when your mother did it to you and you're not his mother.

- Don't expect him to read your mind when it comes to giving you presents. If he used to surprise you but now asks you what you want don't say "Oh, anything will be fine," unless of course anything will be fine. If you want something specific say so. Most men would rather do anything than shop so make it easy for him to give you what you want.

- Expect that those things he used to do occasionally he'll never do again.

He'll never see that the carpet needs to be vacuumed, the dry-cleaning needs to be picked up and the stuff in the back of the refrigerator is old enough to walk. Accept that you have different standards from his and yours are infinitely higher.

- Go out with your girlfriends and don't talk about your boyfriends, husbands or significant others. There are fascinating things happening on the planet, many worthy of deliberation. Familiarity may breed contempt but it doesn't have to breed conversation.

- Remember to treat your partner the way you treat your friends. You wouldn't put up with an abusive friend and you shouldn't accept it in a relationship.

- If you wear your wedding ring and he doesn't, take yours off. People get married to each other.

Follow these simple rules and role with the rigmarole that is inevitable in wedded bliss. And one last thought – don't be too quick to give up your day job.

MEN-O-PAUSE

Take a breath

This is the time for change. Yours, not your daughter's. If she's grown and living on her own, you're just getting used to having time to think before you have to react. You've survived the storm that was childhood and ridden the wave that was adolescence. You've done your best work and now it's time to stop and breathe, assess the experiences you've shared and filed away in that Rolodex of a mother's mind. It's time to prioritize, cast off and hold dear only those things that will help you face the next challenge.

You've probably accumulated a lot of lint and dust that clogs the thinking filter, and while you've been mothering, the world's been spinning out changes. Some you will need to embrace, others reject, but at the least you will need to dump some guilt, give up control, examine tradition and applaud your growth. It's Mom's moment to relish in the wonder that is being female, but we often are our own worst enemies if we don't jettison the junk that we've been too busy to examine.

Start with your responsibilities. How much is really yours and what form does it take? How much have you just assumed because it was easier than getting others to agree with you? Now's the time to prioritize and if you haven't done it yet, feel the weight lift from your shoulders as you shrug them and say to yourself, "from now on I'm going to:

Delegate
and lower my standards.

Know there's nothing better than a lousy meal prepared by somebody else. You're not the only one who can cut, peel, grate, arrange, organize, pot, plant, hemstitch, wash, dry, iron, clean, seat, welcome, scrub, pack, unpack, vacuum, straighten, recycle, sort, bag, polish, shop, sweep, fluff, cure, treat, drive, supervise, instruct, play, prepare, pour, nag, remind, schedule, attend, pay, encourage, soothe, plan and delegate.

Once you begin to delegate, action will have to follow. Chores will have to be charted, responsibilities shared. But be prepared. The open spaces in your daily planners may well be taken up listening to whining about fairness and justice. Just put on your headphones and turn up the radio. Your family will adjust to the fact that:

We are not the only ones capable of:

- putting it in the dishwasher instead of the sink. There is no dish fairy.
- making breakfast that doesn't come in a box.
- dusting or doing anything involving a rag.
- being on bathroom patrol, cleaning the sink and hanging the towels.

- baking a birthday cake and knowing how many candles to put on it.
- setting and clearing the table, scraping, rinsing and putting the dishes in the dishwasher.
- starting dinner without being asked.
- doing a week's worth of grocery shopping in one hour without a list and with a toddler.

- plugging in the vacuum and using it, even that long skinny thing.
- making, frosting, packing, delivering and mailing holiday cookies.
- making sure homework gets done before adult bedtime.
- finding something behind something in the refrigerator, closet or on a shelf.

- nagging kids to clean their rooms and hang up their clothes instead of throwing them down the chute.
- being "chore police" and being sure things get done.
- removing, sloshing, wringing and rinsing cloth diapers.
- changing the linens and making the beds without asking why.

- serving as chauffeur for scout meetings and dance lessons and chaperoning the sleep-over.
- refilling ice trays before you're down to the last cube.
- planting the garden and remembering to water it.
- cutting and arranging flowers just because.

- being "practice police" for the children you've forced to take lessons.
- explaining how sex works before someone else does.
- finding clothes that disappeared in the dryer.
- being the tooth fairy and not forgetting inflation.
- shopping, wrapping, carding, bowing, and tying gifts for others.

But even if you manage to deflect some responsibilities you'll also find there is no one who believes you can do certain types of things and find it rewarding. Why do we have this reputation for not being able to fix anything? Why do we think of ourselves as helpless with a lug wrench or circular saw? When we're adept at using a power tool that isn't a sexual device we're regarded as unfeminine. Cries of "You can do that?" can be heard springing from conversations at PTA meetings and in boardrooms. Why shouldn't we do that?

Do power tools come with "male only" licenses? Of course not, but we've fed the monster ourselves and it's time to hit the hardware store, armed with credit cards and pockets of cash, buy up everything and anything that makes noise and cuts, screws or shapes. We need to teach our daughters about the newfound tools of liberation. They need to see us as capable, industrious and self-reliant. Show her your grit. The only concrete way to do it is by...

Conquering Matter

I have to start the morning with coffee and steamed milk. But when the irreplaceable little rubber gasket on my oh-so-trendy imported Italian steamer wore out, I was forced to heat milk in a common aluminum pan.

Not very '90s. As a further humiliation I had to froth it by rolling the handle of a French whisk between my palms, the same way kids make clay snakes in kindergarten.

Because proper temperature is vital in aluminum pan cooking, I was always careful to stand over it until just that moment when it rose in the pan about to boil over. Only once did I leave it unattended. The milk boiled over the pan and into the stovetop. Since that day the damn burner has not lit. Frustration mounted every time I prepared something requiring heat because I had to compensate for that one burner. I had to reach and stretch, transfer and wait. I'd try it every now and then hoping a miracle had been performed while I slept. Maybe the tooth fairy would want latte before leaving and she'd fix it. It became an annoyance. And every morning I began the day just a little cranky. I replaced the steamer. My coffee improved and so did my disposition, but I still had this faulty, milk-stained, sour-smelling, gas-emitting, useless front burner.

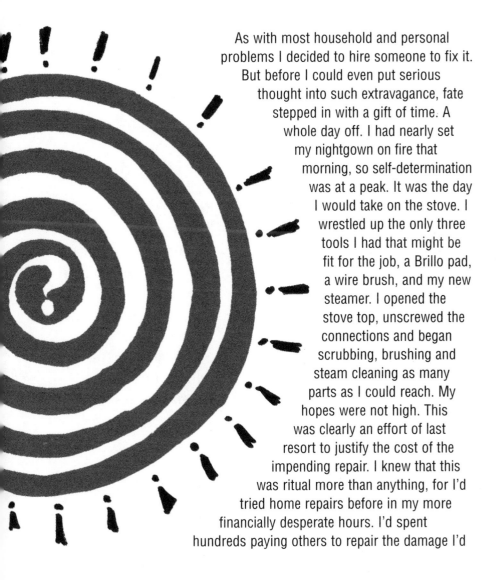

As with most household and personal problems I decided to hire someone to fix it. But before I could even put serious thought into such extravagance, fate stepped in with a gift of time. A whole day off. I had nearly set my nightgown on fire that morning, so self-determination was at a peak. It was the day I would take on the stove. I wrestled up the only three tools I had that might be fit for the job, a Brillo pad, a wire brush, and my new steamer. I opened the stove top, unscrewed the connections and began scrubbing, brushing and steam cleaning as many parts as I could reach. My hopes were not high. This was clearly an effort of last resort to justify the cost of the impending repair. I knew that this was ritual more than anything, for I'd tried home repairs before in my more financially desperate hours. I'd spent hundreds paying others to repair the damage I'd done repairing. That's why I no longer try nearly so hard.

I scrubbed these stove parts until they were the cleanest things about the stove. I put them back under the hood and reassembled the tubing. I lowered the top, and turned the on/off switch with little enthusiasm. My mind was already on the yellow pages.

IT WORKED!

I shrieked at a volume louder than any I would ever accept from my daughter

who was standing near. I grinned a face-breaking grin shining in the dim light of the flame and the blaze of self-adulation. She had a puzzled look on her face as though she were meeting one of my new personalities for the first time. It dawned on me that she had never seen me win an appliance victory before, never seen me bask in the afterglow of household domination. She had never seen me conquer. "That's pathetic," I mumbled to myself and threw in another load of laundry.

Yet just as important to know when to throw in the towel. Even the mightiest of domestic warriors needs to place the occasional call for reinforcements. You know the key to winning is not always winning. Your daughter needs to know that, too. Sometimes, it's just:

Knowing when to give up

Hot bath
Pull plug
Nothing
Dry
Powder
Tub
Water
Standing water
Snake
Bend hair catcher
Standing water
Chemicals
Standing water mixed with
Chemicals
More and different chemicals
Chemical reaction
Standing brown water
Burning eyes
Brown streaks down white tub
Sides
Fumes
Bent metal
Standing acid
Standing
Left standing
I need a bath
I need a plumber

Changing your mindset and habits is hard enough but wait until you take on the rest of America! There is some major finger-pointing going on and women, we are the targets. Well, we have fingers too. Flip one out the next time the accusations push you to the point of threatening. If you don't, your daughter will no doubt hear them twenty years from now. When you hear yourself ready to say:

if I hear one more time...

– how American women are destroying the family by working.
– how divorced women are destroying their children by working.
– how women shouldn't worry about trying to do it all. Stop! Try substituting the word "men" for the word "women" in the above three sentences. Make any sense? Of course not. Doesn't make any sense to blame the women either.

No one would choose to hold down three jobs at one time unless they were crazy. Most moms who work need to and it's not to buy a new car or the latest in French couture. It's to buy macaroni and cheese and new shoes for kids whose feet grow faster than the grass on the front lawn.

Divorced women are one half of the divorced family. The other half, divorced men, often don't have custody, sometimes don't see the kids except to take them for pizza and a movie and millions don't pay child support unless they're taken to court. Sometimes not even then. Of course there are great divorced dads out there. They're great because they're working, doing more than taking the kids for pizza and a movie and paying child support on time.

If Mom doesn't do it all, who's going to do it? Not the divorced dad. That's what divorce means. The kids? They're probably just trying to be kids and expecting them to do more than make the bed, wash a few dishes or run the vacuum occasionally is impractical.

But relax, Mom, because if you've had time to read this far you should know that some research says daughters of working mothers see women as being able to do more things. Small wonder. Seems after the age of seven, those daughters have higher achievement levels and greater aspirations. The same has always been said for boys and their fathers.

Relax.   OK, relaxing time's up.

You've worked all week. The blessed weekend is here and it's time to look forward to some downtime with the family.
The executive washroom is miles away, you're home now. Your impulse is to rule.
Your family expects it. Fight the urge. The following are things for a daughter to know. There's:

EXTRA ★ CREDIT
for the Mom who

knows no one else can do things as well as she does but has them do it anyway.

✔

knows slice-and-bake cookies are just fine and bakes guilt-free.

✖

teaches her daughter how to read food labels but still lets her pick out a few things to buy just because they taste good.

✗

lets the answering machine take the calls sometimes.

☆

buys her daughter ball gloves as well as Barbies.

✍

shares some responsibilities and doesn't just assume them.

✔

understands the house is everyone's home, not just Mom's house.

lets the kids rearrange the furniture once in awhile.

☆

lets her daughter paint her bedroom walls lime green if that's what she wants.

❋

says "I'm not cleaning up your room" and means it.

✌

listens. Doesn't advise, comment on, or suggest. She just listens.

✔

forgets the life lessons on occasion. Not every experience has to have a message.

❀

lets her daughter have a tantrum and occasionally has one of her own.

✕

knows she can't fix everything.

understands that no kid
is going to willingly eat brussel sprouts.

So you're in control because you've given up control. You're feeling pretty good that you're setting the right example. You're leading and your daughter will surely follow. She'll understand that every now and then you need a day to yourself. Not a weekend day. A weekday. It's good for the soul and the stress level. Think about it. No calls, no demands:

No GUILT!

Why, when we get a day off, or take a day off, do we feel we have to accomplish something?
Why do we begin with a chore list seven inches long?
Why do we take a mental inventory at noon about what we should have and didn't do all morning?
Why at the end of the day do we begin to look forward to returning to our jobs?
Why do we need work to save us from the agony we feel about non-accomplishment at home?

Take a day off. Do nothing and at the day's end when you look at your seven-inch list with absolutely no crossouts, say out loud, "So what?"

A DAY OFF

Wash
Clean
Rearrange
File
Fold
Mend
Organize
Eat
Sharpen Pencils
Feel guilty
Phone
Latte
Phone
Phone
More Latte
No washing
No cleaning
No rearranging
No filing
No folding
No mending
No organizing
No guilt

That's right. No guilt about doing something exquisite for yourself. Just this once you're going to spend the money on you instead of new tires. You've steeled your resolve and you're going to indulge in something totally wild. What to choose? A manicure? Too mundane. A mud bath? Too messy. A new outfit? Too practical. It needs to be almost sinful. It turns out to be:

The Herbal Body Scam

The only body that ever needs to be wrapped in herbs is poultry. Don't forget that. Don't be tempted as I was by the thought of exotic spices eking inches off your body like some kind of organic lyposuction.

I can kid about this now because I'm smarter about such issues. It's the kind of smart you get right after you do something really stupid. Like getting an herbal body wrap at a strip mall. I didn't want to of course, I was

approached by a friend. So as women sometimes do, I passed on the invitation to one of my friends as well.

And then there were three. We went to the strip mall, stripped down (so that's where they got the name) to our underpants and stood there while a total stranger layered us with ace bandages. Granted, they were hot herbed ace bandages, but I was feeling oddly like Sunday dinner watching her take these things directly from an old Nesco cooker and wind them around my body.

In all honesty, it was ridiculous. From the wrapping rooms, we walked like accident victims to a series of vibrating tables, bandaged from neck to ankle, soaking wet and wrapped in plastic jumpsuits to trap the heat. We moved from table to table for about an hour, chatting and laughing about how stupid the whole thing was. Here we were, three otherwise intelligent women, actually thinking we could take off pounds without anything but condiments, a little vaporized water and a lot of positive thinking.

They kept us there a good long time, probably part of the mental manipulation to make it seem more legit. When the timer finally went off we weighed and measured out, gently assured by all the women there that we did indeed lose inches, maybe yards. We nodded and smiled in total, wishful agreement but when we checked the mirror it was clear we were idiots—idiots who were now out a lot of money. We wrote our checks for $45 apiece, took our pamphlets and our lumps and headed for the idiot exit. We knew we'd been taken. But we had soft skin and an aroma a Cornish hen would die for.

This experience is not an isolated one. The same principle holds for those places that wire you up, put patches on you where your muscles lie just under the skin's surface and then electrocute the heck out of you in minute jolts. All it does it tighten the muscle. It doesn't make you lose weight but you do measure smaller and you're separated from your $45.00 just as easily.

Beware the anti-wrinkle-any kind-of-cream with exfoliating properties. Or the latest rage, the alpha-hydrox, multi-syllabic stuff that's smeared on your face. Or nail extensions, wraps and other prostheses. Or permanent makeup liner on your lips, eyes or brows. You become what you eat. You are the way you look. If you bite your nails they're short. If you wrinkle, so what? Change your attitude. Your looks will follow. And why deny yourself the chance to be the most gray-haired, short-nailed, plain-faced, full-figured, most well-adjusted gal around?

We allow ourselves to be dragged through a lot of ridiculous machinations because we're conditioned. We believe a lot that isn't true. You're old enough now to cast off what's phony, useless and troublesome but your daughter isn't. She needs to learn to stick society's samples on a slide and put them under a microscope of analytical reasoning to examine the frauds masquerading as facts. Herein lies the challenge for both of you. Examine the thought, reject the assumptions and consider what we call:

Freud Fraud

Sigmund Freud:

Id, ego, superego

pleasure principle

reality principle

ego ideal

sublimation

fixation

repression

regression

projection

female genital deficiency

Around 1939, along came fellow German, Karen Horney: basic anxiety basic hostility rejection of Freud, rejection of penis envy rejection of theory of female inferiority.

She created quite a maelstrom, was alienated from many in her profession and accused of psychoanalytical heresy. If they had identified it back then, they probably would have labeled her "PMSing."

She said women are not mutilated men. Maybe men have "womb envy." Despite her claims, despite the lack of empirical studies Freud remained the "father of psychoanalysis." Karen Horney was relegated to being a ticked-off teacher.

A couple of decades later, Freud's theories were under fire from males and females in the psychology profession.

Penis Envy? I don't think so. Question authority. Question theory. Questions?

Answers. Have one ready at all times, women, because you never know when you're going to have need of a snappy retort. You may find the biggest battles fought in the most unlikely places. Like sports bars. Oh yes, it's a troublesome spot where the sparring has to be done with words. You need to sharpen your wit, grab your thesaurus and have at tongue a quick reply when you hear some idiot insult the linebacker on the television by screaming:

He runs like a girl!

Winter in Wisconsin. While some are off skiing and skating the rest of us are in search of more sedentary recreation. Watching the local pro football team, for example. Our beloved Packers. We don ourselves in green and gold, cheeseheads and helmets and do as many good fans do in these parts, meet at nearby taverns and experience each sports moment together.

When last we did just this we were reminded of the clearly drawn lines some of these places enjoy. Lines of separation. Lines of segregation. Lines that define what women do and what men do. Lines that define the holders of the deeds.

Four women and one man made it to the game this Sunday. We never know just who will show, but all are welcome and greeted like long-lost friends. We sat in the front, just feet away from the big screen and the sign that reprimanded, "No dancing on the tables." This was strictly upheld from all indications.

Behind us were three or four tables of men, all pumped up in athletic wear, with loud boomy voices and heavy fists. At first our table ignored theirs and vice versa. Past half-time, and this applies to sobriety as well,

things got really loud. Whenever a player would make a lame play one table of men would shout out, "You play like a girl," or "You run like a woman." I doubt they were thinking of Jackie Joyner-Kersey.

This began to annoy us. But it was not until, "You pussy!" bellowed out of a mouth and ricocheted off the trophies that we finished our drinks and left. The Neanderthals won the room and the proprietors lost our business. Maybe a sign should have been hung stating, "Insulting language will not be tolerated." Maybe the wait-person could have reminded them they weren't the only ones in the room and perhaps they weren't using their best judgment. Maybe, but she didn't say a word. Maybe we should have approached the table and politely informed them we were offended and asked them to refrain. Maybe we should have discussed it with the management, or at least informed them that we were leaving, taking our money with us and planning never to return. Woulda coulda shoulda. We didn't.

No one did anything until one of us yelled at the top of our lungs as we left, "Scrotum!!!"

Childish, yes. But as shallow a response as it was, we thought it probably translated well.

Silent protest and physical assertiveness works well in more refined situations. Consider that once you are enlightened your intellectual thirst will lead to questioning all sorts of conventional thought. With dogged persistence you can even challenge the simplest assumptions such as who has sovereignty over:

THE ARMREST

We have a wonderful new-old theater here in our town. One that used to be grand and arrogant, with snobbish narrow seats and aisles only wide enough for still feet. I love the theater but only go on what my mom would call, "fancy occasions." Fancy occasions are those public outings requiring physical discomfort and parking ramps. My daughter and I have made a traditional fancy occasion of attending *A Christmas Carol*. Traditions are good. Our tradition is for me to yell about a half-hour before curtain that it's time to go. Then the tradition is for us to get in the car, stop at a cash machine and run out of time. This way we can maintain our tradition of speeding through downtown to get to the theater by show time. It brings us so much closer together.

This year, we whisked in with the lowering of the lights. Between us, we had one aisle seat ticket, so our entrance was quick. My daughter vied for the aisle and won, as children so often do in public places. I got to sit next to the big Norseman probably named after an explorer. He looked oversized for the seat he was given, like a Ken doll sitting on a Weeblo chair. In his defense, the seats in this theater are small and the armrests skinny.

I didn't have a chance at it, nor should I have had coming in late and all. But between the first "Bah Humbug" and the ghost of Christmas past what surfaced as a minor irritation grew into a great big thing. I wondered why the Norseman didn't slide his arm up or down to expose some small bit of wood for my elbow to rest on. I wondered why he didn't verbally acknowledge the fact that he had laid silent claim to the only island of arm refuge and would swap with me at intermission. I wondered why he didn't realize his leg had fallen into my leg space.

I moved my leg over a bit so that it would rub right against his and just as I planned, he moved his leg quickly but not far enough. I inched my leg to his again. Again he moved. It was a simple victory, but I was going for the wood.

Curtain. The Norseman got up to stretch and walk the center aisle. As my daughter and I stood to let him pass, I grinned and shifted to the right for the approach. I sat down with my arm bent ready to assume the position, which I did with quite a flourish. The seats never felt wider. I savored every minute of the fifteen-minute intermission, and waited for his return. I wondered what he would do. I wondered what I would do. As my daughter and I stood to let him in I knew I would have to swoop down and under to beat him back to the armrest. I had rehearsed it while he was gone so I moved like a ballerina. He sat. I left my arm draped across the rest, as his had been for the last hour with no movement, no words, no look. He shifted in his seat a bit, raised both arms...and crossed them over his chest. I looked over at him all piled up like custard on a cone. "That was pretty easy," I thought, removing my elbow and putting my hands in my lap. It was a great second act.

Response in any positive form beats internalizing. Who knows what conversations will spring up if we speak out.
The problem is gender sensitivity comes most often when threats ring out in the halls of justice.
That's what happened here and that's why the edict came down;

Zip Up *Snap-On*

The story crossed the AP wire and read:

"Wrenching Decision: Snap-On Tools Drops its Girlie Calendars

(Kenosha)– A 12-year legacy is coming to a close for a Kenosha Tool-Maker.

Though largely unknown to a wider audience, Snap-On Tools Calendars have become a legend of sorts in repair shops and factories around the country. For more than a decade, Snap-On has sent out more than one (M) million calendars that feature scantily clad females promoting the company's tools.

A spokesman says: 'We felt our customers were looking for an image boost.' So it dropped the calendars in favor of a two (M) million dollar homespun advertising campaign promoting the virtues of mechanics.

Snap-On denies that it killed its calendar out of fears of sexual-harassment claims. It says its calendar was tamer than many, its models were never nude and actually put on more clothes over the years."

A land mine of controversy. Right there, neatly wrapped up in an innocuous enough idea – a calendar. There's the argument that nearly naked women have no place on a calendar, pumping mechanic's tools. That it's sexist, stereotypical, demeaning. You know the argument. But if you accept that premise then you have to accept the idea those "hunk" calendars are equally as problematic, demeaning, etc. and that no self-respecting female of the '90s would use one. Doesn't wash. What's wrong with looking at beautiful bodies, male or female, fantasizing with full-color objects of lust? Does it really demean anyone? Does it really mean women or men are regarded only as sex objects? Some would say of course not, but the problem comes when the women or the men are used purely for sexual excitement and have nothing to do with the product sold.

I started to think about the last time I saw a calendar like Snap-On's and realized I'm not really the audience for such things because the time I spend hanging out in auto repair shops is limited. I had lost track of advertising and couldn't imagine any company would still be using half-naked "babes" in high heels to sell garden tractors and lug wrenches. It appeared as if while I wasn't looking, Snap-On had been holding on to a tradition I thought long dead.

So now my senses were awakened and I started seeing fleshy torsos everywhere. In television there were bath soap commercials where seemingly naked women, men and children were counting wet body parts. In Calvin Klein ads everything was shot on a beach in the surf and no one had on clothes, which is what I think they were selling. Provocatively dressed women with sultry smiles standing beside the latest model LX-Whatever, trying to sell you the car of the future today.

Once I started looking, I found it everywhere. Soap operas opened with video of penetrating kisses to naked body spaces and champagne corks exploding from bottles that were overtly phallic. When I used that same video in a story on which I was working, some colleagues were outraged at the seven seconds and disbelieving when I told them it aired every afternoon at the beginning of a soap opera and no one ever complained.

The night the Snap-On calendar died, there were jokes about it and a story in the newscast, done by a male reporter who was genuinely confused over whether to call the women in the calendar "calendar girls" or the "women in the calendar." He canvassed the newsroom looking for guidance. I voted for the latter and lost.

But the most telling comment came from a producer who said she remembered when "men had their calendars, women had their cookbooks and it was a simpler time." She, of course, was right. There had been simpler times when women stayed home, cooked, cleaned and raised the children. Men went off to the office, the garage, the factory or wherever they went. It was a segregated society wearing a smile and an apron.

But now women go to the office, men help raise the children, buy as many cookbooks as women and take more cooking classes. Women work in garages and factories.

It is a more complex time.

So long Snap-On.

With the death of one tradition comes the renewed popularity of another. Bumper stickers are a curiously American phenomenon and we are currently experiencing a bumper crop of bumper opinions. Although face to face debate may be the richer experience, any communication must be better than none, so let's make the best of it, bad grammar and all. Let's find joy in our differences and applaud our common bonds. We've proven for centuries that we can respect each other's choices even when it makes for:

STICKY BUMPERS

I have a friend who drives a beat-up old Honda station wagon that starts even when it's 60° below. On the dated and dented chromed back bumper is a sticker that's been there for years. It reads "Against Abortion? Don't Have One!"

She drove her trusty car up to the gas pump one day, stuck the nozzle into the side of the car and pumped in the cheapest, lowest octane fuel they had.

Staring off into space while the gas flowed in she barely noticed the woman who drove up to the pump opposite her, facing the other direction. This woman was harried, loudly slamming the door on her coat-tail, loosening it with a disgusted look, then unscrewing the gas cap and jamming the nozzle into the opening. She looked up at my friend; their eyes met for one nano-second but not recognizing each other both looked down without speaking.

That's when each spied the other's bumper sticker. Just across the asphalt from "Against Abortion: Don't Have One!" was "I'm Pro-Life and I Vote."

It took a moment for the message to register with each of them, their philosophies on life conflicting in a few words inked on plastic and stuck to the rear-end of a car.

The other woman finished her task, paid her bill, got into the driver's seat, punched a number on her car phone and pulled away into traffic.

My friend finished up, fell back into her well-worn spot and reached over to be sure the baby was in her car seat and securely belted in the back. She found drive on the gear shift, checked the rear view mirror and drove off.

Two people living their consciences, each going her own way. Women quietly accepting loud differences.

CONCLUSION

Monarchies. Daughters need them. Daughters need us. We are the only things standing between them and the standup-sitcom-moms of commercial television.

Today's mothers are as mothers have always been. We are the warm hands, welcoming voices, the shoulders and ears and gentle pushes. We are also executives, lawmakers, newsmakers, employees and the greatest agents of change. We're at home, on the road, on-line and we're raising daughters who need our experience and wisdom.

So, if you have a daughter, get out the sensible shoes and dump those rose-colored glasses. There's a lot of ground to cover on a terrain demanding clear vision. It will be a joyride from the delivery room to the board room, from cradle to college and beyond.

If you are a daughter, may you never suffer humiliation, frustration or discrimination. If it comes your way, may you know how to confront, question and negotiate change.

And always remember this:

Mothers have the last word,
The last thought
And the last laugh.

And that's the way it should be.